The Golden Text of A.A.

God, the Pioneers, and Real Spirituality

Other Titles by Dick B.

Dr. Bob and His Library

Anne Smith's Journal, 1933-1939:
  A.A.'s Principles of Success

The Oxford Group & Alcoholics Anonymous:
  A Design for Living That Works

The Akron Genesis of Alcoholics Anonymous

New Light on Alcoholism:
  God, Sam Shoemaker, and A.A.

The Books Early AAs Read for Spiritual Growth

Courage to Change (with Bill Pittman)

The Good Book and The Big Book:
  A.A.'s Roots in the Bible

That Amazing Grace:
  The Role of Clarence and Grace S. in Alcoholics Anonymous

Good Morning!:
  Quiet Time, Morning Watch, Meditation, and Early A.A.

Turning Point:
  A History of A.A.'s Spiritual Roots and Successes

HOPE!: The Story of Geraldine D., Alina Lodge & Recovery

Utilizing Early A.A.'s Spiritual Roots for Recovery Today

By the Power of God:
  A Guide to Early A.A. Groups & Forming Similar Groups Today

The Golden Text of A.A.

God, the Pioneers, and Real Spirituality

Dick B.

Paradise Research Publications, Inc.
Kihei, Maui, Hawaii

Paradise Research Publications, Inc., P.O. Box 837, Kihei, HI 96753-0837

This Paradise Research Publications, Inc., Edition is published by arrangement with Good Book Publishing Company, P.O. Box 837, Kihei, HI 96753-0837

Cover Design: Lili Crawford (Maui Cyber Design)

The publication of this volume does not imply affiliation with nor approval or endorsement from Alcoholics Anonymous World Services, Inc.

Publisher's Cataloging in Publication

B., Dick.
    The Golden Text of A.A. : God, the Pioneers, and Real Spirituality / Dick. B.
    p. cm.
    Preassigned LCCN: 99-93045
    ISBN: 1-885803-29-X

Contents

1 We Will Tell You about   1

2 What Early AAs Thought about God Almighty   5
   The Pioneers Believed in God   5
   The Pioneers Understood Who God Is   10
      God Was Not Some Ill-defined "Higher Power" . .   10
      Change, Compromise, and Fear of Being
         "God Bitten"   12
      Biblical Names for God They Used   16
   Willing Unbelievers Came to Believe in God   19
      John 7:17 and Willingness   19
      Obedience and Knowledge   20
      There Was A Reward   21
      Action As the Key to Belief   22
   The Pioneers Believed That, When Sought, God Heals   22
      Their Bible and God's Healings   23
      Bill W.'s Inaccurate and Incomplete Description
         of A.A. Sources   26
      Bill's Own Writings Continued the Original
         Emphasis on God   33
      Bill's Revealing Remarks to Father John C.
         Ford, S.J.   35
      Bill's Alleged Four A.A. Sources Revisited   36

3 Their Path, Jesus Christ, and a Relationship with God .   41
   Steps Along the Path   42
   The Miraculous Result   43
      How They Expressed the Result   43
      The Message They Formulated and Preached   45
      The Continued Challenge to Do God's Will   50
      Principles and Power   52

4 The Golden Text of A.A. They Adopted   55
   The Golden Text   55
   As Christian believers, AAs Could Claim Power
        through Accepting Christ   57
   Jesus Promised God's Power to All Who
        Believed, Saying: 58
   The Pioneers Claimed Receipt of That Power   59
   Giving God the Glory   60
   Expressing Gratitude through Deed and Word   61

5 The Critical Need to Seek God Again Today   63
   Self-help Will Not Cut It. That Is Not a Solution. . . .   64
   Medical Help and Psychological Help Have Not Cut It   65
   The Four Early A.A. Factors Needed Today   66
        First, A Fellowship of Those Needing Help   67
        Second, a Healing and Cure by God Almighty . . .   69
        Third, a Program That Changes Lives   73
        Fourth, a Message of Victory to Carry   75

6 Two Challenges for Real Spirituality Today   77
   The Challenges   77
   The Real Meaning of "Spirituality" in Early A.A. and for
        Today   78

1

We Will Tell You about . . .

The Pioneer AAs—those who joined the program in its formative years before the Big Book was published in 1939—knew where to get help for their seemingly hopeless and progressive disease of mind and body. They were, some said, "medically incurable."

Self-knowledge had failed them.[1] Willpower had failed them.[2] Fear had done nothing but defeat them.[3] In fact, they concluded that probably no human power could help them.[4] At least two of

---

[1] *Alcoholics Anonymous*, 3rd ed. (New York: Alcoholics Anonymous World Services, Inc., 1976), p. 7: "Surely this was the answer—self-knowledge. But it was not, for the frightful day came when I drank once more." See also pp. 36-37, 39. Hereafter this title will usually be referred to as the Big Book, a registered trademark of Alcoholics Anonymous World Services, Inc.

[2] Big Book, p. 5: "I saw I could not take so much as one drink. I was through forever. Before then, I had written lots of sweet promises, but my wife happily observed that this time I meant business. And so I did. Shortly afterward I came home drunk. There had been no fight. Where had been my high resolve?" See also pp. 5-6, 21-24.

[3] Big Book, p. 8: "Trembling, I stepped from the hospital a broken man. Fear sobered me for a bit. Then came the insidious insanity of that first drink, and on Armistice Day 1934, I was off again." See p. 151: ". . . the hideous Four Horsemen—Terror, Bewilderment, Frustration, Despair. Unhappy drinkers who read this page will understand."

[4] Big Book, p. 60: "That probably no human power could have relieved our alcoholism."

1

them were told by a renowned physician: "there is no doubt in my mind that you were 100% hopeless apart from Divine help.[5]

These real alcoholics of the 1930's were therefore in no mood to seek relief in a "self-help" movement—the group therapy or mutual self-help idea that seems to occupy the spotlight in the Twelve Step recovery field today.[6] As a matter of fact, that idea had been rejected as a cure by Bill Wilson's spiritual mentor, the Reverend Sam Moor Shoemaker, Jr., in a title Shoemaker wrote about three years before Wilson first sought Sam's help in 1934. Shoemaker wrote:

> In the preceding sermon we spoke of the central importance of the Cross of Christ in the faith and experience of a Christian. We said that what God did for us on the Cross is a fountain of inexhaustible blessing and power, and that faith in the Cross is the cure and corrective for the gospel of "self-help," so common today even amongst believers, which centers in the effort of the human will toward self-improvement.[7]

The great bulk of A.A.'s forty pioneers—who authorized their basic recovery text as a means of telling others how they had been delivered—had an understanding of God. They had sought a relationship with Him and learned of a plan for doing His will. They realized the Bible was the basic source for information. And

---

[5]Big Book, p. 43.

[6]See *The Self-Help Sourcebook: Your Guide to Community and Online Support Groups, Sixth Edition* (Denville, NJ: American Self-Help Clearinghouse, 1998). Hundreds of societies, including Alcoholics Anonymous, are so labeled in this reference work and in many bookstores today. See also Herbert Fingarette, *Heavy Drinking: The Myth of Alcoholism As a Disease* (Berkeley: University of California Press, 1988), p. 87: "The A.A. model has also had enormous influence on the organization of self-help groups for relatives and children of alcoholics and for gamblers, overeaters, and others whose behavior seems to fit the 'addictive' pattern;" George E. Vaillant, *The Natural History of Alcoholism Revisited* (Cambridge, MA: Harvard University Press, 1995), p. 267; Terry Webb, *Tree of Renewed Life: Spiritual Renewal of the Church through the Twelve-Step Program* (New York: Crossroad, 1992), p. 120.

[7]Samuel M. Shoemaker, Jr., *If I Be Lifted Up: Thoughts About the Cross* (New York: Fleming H. Revell, 1931), p. 167.

studied it! They also learned that the First Century Christian Fellowship (also known as the Oxford Group) and the teachings of Sam Shoemaker, the Group's chief American lieutenant, offered to them a plan for removing from their lives the blocks to God and for a right relationship with God and other believers. Then, consistent with the Bible and the Oxford Group's witnessing emphasis, they sought to pass on what *they* had received. And they found that when they gave, they received.

This booklet contains a factual account of what the pioneers believed, how they established their relationship with God, the miraculous results they obtained through the power of God, and the manner in which they appropriately expressed their gratitude to God. And they used a phraseology which Bill Wilson introduced, A.A. Number Three (Bill Dotson) endorsed and labeled, and Dr. Bob had always espoused. It was called the Golden Text of A.A. And we think it will give direction to your thoughts about A.A.'s Big Book, Twelve Steps, and Fellowship.

2

What Early AAs Thought about God Almighty

As the Reverend Sam Shoemaker often wrote (about *believing)*, one should *begin with what he or she does believe, not with* what he or she *does not believe*. Believing is an integral part of the human thinking process. What one believes usually determines what one does. And, in the A.A. thought process, AAs did not start their program of recovery with what they did not believe. They started with what they did believe or were willing to believe. They did this so they could come to believe in a power—the power of Almighty God—that would set them free from their obsession, delusion, and illusion. A cunning *spirit* that had left them without power to seek any real solution to life other than the solution of liquor. A liquor solution that was driving them to death, insanity, and imprisonment (whether physical, mental, or spiritual).

The Pioneers Believed in God

Early AAs believed in God. They had to. No human power could help them, they declared. In the first draft of their original basic text, they used words quite different from those you will see in today's Big Book text. They wrote:

Our description of the alcoholic, the chapter to the agnostic, and
our personal adventures before and after, have been designed to
sell you three pertinent ideas: (a) That you are alcoholic and
cannot manage your own life. (b) That probably no human
power can relieve your alcoholism. (c) *That God can and will.*
If you are not convinced on these vital issues, you ought to re-
read the book to this point or else throw it away![1]

They also said such things as:

God has to work twenty-four hours a day in and through us, or
we perish.[2]

Each individual, in the personal stories, describes in his own
language and from his own point of view the way he found or
rediscovered God.[3]

Our ideas did not work. But the God idea did.[4]

Actually we were fooling ourselves, for deep down in every
man, woman, and child is the fundamental idea of God.[5]

God had restored his sanity. What is this but a miracle of
healing? Yet its elements are simple. Circumstances made him
willing to believe. He humbly offered himself to his Maker--
then he knew. Even so has God restored us all to our right
minds.[6]

---

[1]*The Big Book of Alcoholics Anonymous: A copy of the original manuscript Published
by Works Publishing Co.*, 17 William St., Newark N.J., p. 17. A reproduction bearing
the following statement by Dr. Bob's sponsee Clarence H. Snyder: "This is a copy of
the original manuscript before later changes were made. This is the original Big Book."

[2]Original manuscript, *supra*, p. 7.

[3]Original manuscript, *supra*, p. 13.

[4]Original manuscript, *supra*, p. 23.

[5]Original manuscript, *supra*, p. 24.

[6]Original manuscript, *supra*, p. 25

But there is One who has all power--That One is God. You must find Him now![7]

Get down upon your knees and say to your Maker, as you understand Him: "God, I offer myself to Thee. . . ."[8]

In this book you read again and again that God did for us what we could not do for ourselves.[9]

You have been trying to get a new attitude, a new relationship with your Creator, and to discover the obstacles in your path.[10]

God will constantly disclose more to you and to us. Ask him in your morning meditation what you can do each day for the man who is still sick.[11]

The foregoing are only a few examples of the original references to God Almighty, the Creator, the Maker. They make it abundantly clear that the A.A. pioneers believed in God. They had little choice. Quoting Bill's spiritual teacher Sam Shoemaker almost verbatim, they felt compelled to write:

When we became alcoholics, crushed by a self-imposed crisis we could not postpone or evade, we had to fearlessly face the proposition that either God is everything or else He is nothing. God either is, or He isn't. What was our choice to be?[12]

Just a couple of years before A.A. was born, Shoemaker had written:

---

[7]Original manuscript, *supra*, p. 26.

[8]Original manuscript, *supra*, p. 28.

[9]Original manuscript, *supra*, p. 32.

[10]Original manuscript, *supra*, p. 33.

[11]Original manuscript, *supra*, p. 74.

[12]Original manuscript, *supra*, p. 24.

But we may be wrong. Faith is not sight: it is a high gamble. There are only two alternatives here. God is, or He isn't. You leap one way or the other. It is a risk to take to bet everything you have on God. So is it a risk not to.[13]

A.A. co-founder Dr. Bob made it clear which choice had to be made. From his standpoint, it was the *only* choice if you wanted what A.A. had to offer. Dr. Bob had the following colloquy with his sponsee Clarence Snyder just before Clarence was discharged from the hospital, never to drink again over a period of almost fifty years:

Then he [Dr. Bob] asked [Clarence Snyder], "Do you believe in God, young fella?" [Clarence added] (He always called me "young fella." When he called me Clarence, I knew I was in trouble.)

What does that have to do with it?

Everything, he said.

I guess I do.

Guess, nothing. Either you do or you don't.

Yes, I do.

That's fine, Dr. Bob replied, Now we're getting someplace. All right, get out of bed and on your knees. We're going to pray.[14]

Both of A.A.'s founders personally underlined the importance of belief in God in order to have sanity restored and to recover.

---

[13]Samuel M. Shoemaker, Jr., *Confident Faith* (New York: Fleming H. Revell, 1932), p. 187.

[14]*DR. BOB and the Good Oldtimers* (New York: Alcoholics Anonymous World Services, Inc., 1980), p. 144.

Just as soon as the Big Book manuscript was complete, Dr. Bob's personal story appeared first in the personal story section. It has remained in every edition of the Big Book since that time. Dr. Bob said:

> If you think you are an atheist, an agnostic, a skeptic, or have any other form of intellectual pride which keeps you from accepting what is in this book [the Big Book], I feel sorry for you. . . . Your Heavenly Father will never let you down![15]

Many AAs have probably been surprised to learn, from the author's books, that Bill Wilson, a former self-styled "conservative atheist," used the following words when he was speaking (many years after A.A. had been founded) to T. Henry and Clarace Williams, in whose home in Akron the early A.A. meetings were held:

> God knows we've been simple enough and gluttonous enough to get this way, but once we got this way [became real alcoholics], it was a form of lunacy which only God Almighty could cure.[16]

The history of A.A., (as far as the author has finally been able to unravel it to this point in time) is therefore very clear that the pioneers of A.A. and their co-founders Bill Wilson and Dr. Bob believed in the God Almighty who is the author and subject of the Holy Bible they studied so carefully in order to develop their basic ideas for the recovery program.

---

[15]Original manuscript, *supra*, p. 6 of Personal Stories.

[16]See Dick B., *The Akron Genesis of Alcoholics Anonymous*, 2d ed. (Kihei, HI: Paradise Research Publications, Inc., 1998), p. 13. The quote of Bill's statement is taken from a transcript at A.A. General Service Archives in New York. The transcript is of Bill Wilson's December 12, 1954 interview of T. Henry and Clarace Williams in their Akron, Ohio home.

The Pioneers Understood Who God Is

God Was Not Some Ill-defined "Higher Power"

A.A.'s Conference Approved literature of today, as well as many of the commentaries and guides to A.A. and its Steps, wander all over the map when it comes to speaking of the "power" which used to be so plainly called *God.* The absurd names which A.A. itself has given to some nebulous "higher power" defy belief when one knows what the founders and their basic text actually wrote and said about God.[17]

We will not cover or document the weird descriptions which A.A. literature of today, treatment centers, writers, historians, and scholars have given the powerless "power" which is supposed to save a helpless alcoholic.[18] We have documented that in detail elsewhere.[19] But it is appropriate to mention that this power has been called an "It," a "Him, Her, or It," a "tree," a "chair," a "stone," a "doorknob," a "lightbulb," the "goddess," "good,"

---

[17]See Clarence Snyder, *My Higher Power The Lightbulb* (Altamonte Springs, FL: Stephen Foreman, 1985); Dick B., *That Amazing Grace: The Role of Clarence and Grace S. in Alcoholics Anonymous* (San Rafael, CA: Paradise Research Publications, 1996), pp. 46-50.

[18]See Wally P., *Back to Basics: The Alcoholics Anonymous "Beginners' Classes"* (Tucson, AZ: Faith With Works Publishing Company, 1997), pp. 38-39: "As we said earlier, Alcoholics Anonymous is not a religious program. We're free to call this Power anything we wish, as long as it is a Power greater than ourselves. The "Big Book" authors use many different names for this Power including Creative Intelligence, Universal Mind, Spirit of Nature, Czar of the Heavens, Creator, Father of Light and the Great Reality, among others. Quite a few times they call this Power, God, but they use the word God merely for expedience rather than for any religious purpose. Please refer to this Power by any name you believe in or feel comfortable with."

[19]Dick B., *The Oxford Group & Alcoholics: A Design for Living that Works*, 2d ed. (Kihei, HI: Paradise Research Publications, Inc., 1998), pp. 152-58; *The Good Book and The Big Book: A.A.'s Roots in the Bible*, Bridge Builders ed. (Kihei, HI: Paradise Research Publications, Inc., 1997), pp. 53-54. See also, Ernest Kurtz, *Not-God: A History of Alcoholics Anonymous*, exp. ed. (Center City, MN: Hazelden, 1991), p. 50: "The fundamental message of Alcoholics Anonymous, proclaimed by the very presence of a former compulsive drunk standing sober, ran: '*Something saves*'" (emphasis added).

"good orderly direction," "group of drunks," "the group," "Santa Claus," "something," and even "Ralph." You can easily locate these absurdities in today's literature, or you can hear them in A.A. meetings and treatment centers in the United States and elsewhere.[20] The author has personally seen or heard them all in such a manner. Just take a look at these present-day, Conference Approved, A.A. comments:

> While some members prefer to call this Power "God," we were told that this was purely a matter of personal interpretation; we could conceive of the Power in any terms we thought fit [See *This is AA...an introduction to the AA recovery program* (New York: Alcoholics Anonymous World Services, Inc., 1984), p. 15.]

> However, everyone defines this power as he or she wishes. Many people call it God, others think it is the A.A. group, still others don't believe in it at all [See *a Newcomer asks...* (New York: Alcoholics Anonymous World Services, Inc., n.d.), p. 4.]

> Some choose the A.A. group as their "Higher Power"; some look to God as they understand Him; and others rely upon entirely different concepts [See *Members of the Clergy ask about Alcoholics Anonymous*, Rev. ed (New York: Alcoholics Anonymous World Services, Inc., 1992), p. 13.]

> G.O.D., which I define as "Good Orderly Direction," has never let me down. . . . (See *Daily Reflections: A Book of Reflections by A.A. members for A.A. members* (New York: Alcoholics Anonymous World Services, Inc., 1990), p. 79.]

---

[20]Webb, *Tree of Renewed Life*, *supra*, pp. 116-17: "It doesn't matter what your Higher Power is, as long as it works to keep you sober. It could even be that light bulb over there." This concept of Higher Power was introduced at a recent AA meeting by the speaker for the evening. So stated author Webb.

> I couldn't accept the concept of a Higher Power because I
> believed God was cruel and unloving. In desperation I chose a
> table, a tree, then my A.A. group, as my Higher Power (See
> *Daily Reflections, supra*, p. 175.)

> I think that one of the great advantages of my faith in God is
> that I do not understand Him, or Her, or It (See *Daily
> Reflections, supra*, p. 334.)

Dr. Bob never, as far as the author has been able to discover,
referred to God Almighty—the God who is the subject of the Good
Book (as Dr. Bob called it)—by any of the ridiculous names set
forth above.

Change, Compromise, and Fear of Being "God Bitten"

Even during his early, eager sales efforts, Bill Wilson spoke
primarily of God. Only then did he stray with references to a
Higher Power (with capital letters), a Power greater than ourselves
(with capital letters), the group, and Good. A.A.'s official
biography of Bill contains this account:

> Dr. Howard, a psychiatrist in Montclair, New Jersey, made a
> vitally important contribution. . . . Dr. Howard read [the
> manuscript] and brought it back the next day. . . . He said Bill
> was making a damn big mistake. "This is the Oxford Group,"
> he said. "You have to change the whole damn thing." . . .
> "You have to take out the God—the complete God."[21]

Clearly, Bill did *not* take out "the complete God." But he certainly
made changes and compromises by deleting the reference to God
in his proposed Step Two; by adding the Oxford Group phrase
"God as we understood Him" in Steps Three and Eleven; and later
by talking about a "Higher Power" [with capital letters], then "the
group," and then even "good." Using the phrase "higher power,"

---

[21]*Pass It On* (New York: Alcoholics Anonymous World Services, Inc., p. 204).

Bill followed the lead of William James, the Oxford Group, and at least one "new thought" writer.[22] In this respect, however, Bill was not consistent in his grammatical treatment of the phrase. He used the phrase "higher Power" in the Original Manuscript; but he handled it as "higher Power" in once place, and "Higher Power" in the second reference—in the same breath—speaking *God* (See Original Manuscript, pp. 19, 45). This practice was followed by the Oxford Group writers and by Ralph Waldo Trine, the new thought writer.

Bill seemed at this time to be developing a new approach, adopting language found in the literature of Professor William James and in the "act as if" philosophy of the Reverend Sam Shoemaker. Despite his initial decision for Christ at Calvary Rescue Mission and his "hot flash experience" with the "God of the preachers" at Towns Hospital, Bill came to believe that if you started with any of the strange words for "a god" that we have previously cited, you could and would somehow wind up with a knowledge of *God*. Provided, thought Bill, that you took the Steps. And Bill began elaborating on his theory as time passed. Thus in an invited greeting to members of Dutch Groups (of A.A.) attending their Tenth Anniversary Conference at The Hague, in Holland, Bill wrote an article reprinted in the *Exchange Bulletin*:

> One can, for example, surely believe that his own A.A. group is a "higher power." If one's group represents more sobriety and more happiness than the newcomer has, then his group is certainly a "higher power." For the time being the "higher power" can be his own group. And his group is certainly something he can depend upon. We have happily discovered

---

[22]For possible sources of this phrase, see William James, (called by Wilson a "founder" of A.A.) *The Varieties of Religious Experience* (New York: Vintage Books/The Library of America, 1990), p. 429—*higher power*; Victor C. Kitchen (a Wilson friend, Shoemaker associate, and Oxford Group writer), *I Was a Pagan* (New York: Harper & Brothers, 1934), p. 85—*Higher Power*; Ralph Waldo Trine (considered by some to be a "new thought" writer), *In Tune with the Infinite*, 1933 ed. (Indianapolis: The Bobbs-Merrill Company, 1933), p, 199—*Higher Power*.

that when a newcomer commences to take this attitude and he becomes willing to practice the rest of the Twelve Steps, the result is almost always excellent. At the end of a few months, of such an open-minded effort, or after a year at most, our friend finds himself not only sober, but so transformed in his own personal life, that he realizes that neither he or his group could, without God, have accomplished such a miraculous change.

Bill Wilson said it (long after A.A. was founded), but that does not make it so. For A.A. statistics show that one-third of all newcomers are out of the door within ninety days and that fifty percent of all newcomers are gone by the end of a year. The author will let someone else argue that a biblical faith in God Almighty can or cannot arise out of Bill's *group* theory. The author's own observation is that when that "higher power" theory is mixed with New Age and a hundred other religious and spiritual ideas, people announce in A.A. meetings—not what *they* did—but that *you* can believe anything you want or nothing at all. And that is what Conference Approved literature tells them today. This is a far cry from Dr. Bob's Heavenly Father comment on page 181 of the Third Edition of the Big Book.

Contending some ten years after A.A. began that things had changed in A.A., even in the 1940's, Bill stated the following in his address to the American Psychiatric Association at its annual meeting, held in Quebec, May, 1949:

> *Of course we speak little of conversion nowadays because so many people really dread being God-bitten.* But conversion, as broadly described by [William] James, does seem to be our basic process; all other devices are but the foundation.[23]

Bill Wilson simply did not talk this way when he first desperately sought sobriety. He went to the altar at Calvary Rescue

---

[23]*Three Talks to Medical Societies by Bill W., Co-Founder of Alcoholics Anonymous* (New York: Alcoholics Anonymous World Services, Inc., n.d.), p. 31 (emphasis added).

Mission in New York and accepted Jesus Christ as his Lord and Savior. He proclaimed he had been "born again" for sure.[24] When he had his famous "hot flash" experience at Towns Hospital, he called on the "Great Physician" (a name for Jesus). He then concluded he had been in the presence of "The God of the preachers."[25] From his "sponsor" Ebby Thacher, Bill had previously heard that Ebby had made a surrender at Calvary Rescue Mission. Ebby very specifically told Bill that God had done for Ebby what Ebby could not do for himself. Ebby told Bill to surrender to God as Bill *then understood God*.[26] And he inevitably heard either directly from the Rev. Sam Shoemaker or from Shoemaker through Ebby that he (Bill) needed no sophisticated or theological understanding of God to make a surrender. He needed only to get on his knees and surrender as much of himself as he understood to as much of God as he understood.[27] And when Bill went to Akron, he was exposed to the same idea—that one should surrender as much of himself as he knows to as much of God as he knows.[28]

---

[24]See Dick B., *The Akron Genesis of Alcoholics Anonymous*, 2d ed., pp. 326-28.

[25]Dick B., *The Akron Genesis of Alcoholics Anonymous, supra*, pp. 327-28.

[26]Big Book, 3rd ed., p. 13.

[27]See Samuel M. Shoemaker, *Children of the Second Birth* (New York: Fleming H. Revell, 1927), p. 25: "So he said that he would 'surrender as much of himself as he could, to as much of Christ as he understood.' It would be far better if we would let men begin their discipleship where they honestly can, letting their experiences develop until their theology comes straight, rather than cramming a creed down fellows' throats and thinking that it means anything to swallow it whole without digesting it. I quote now from his diary: 'Before I left, we got down on our knees in prayer together—a new and wonderful Christian experience for me—and I dedicated my life not only to belief in Jesus Christ, but to His life and work. . . . I do feel reborn, born of the Spirit.'" See also p. 47.

[28]See Dick B., *Anne Smith's Journal, 1933-1939: A.A.'s Principles of Success*, 3rd ed (Kihei, HI: Paradise Research Publications, Inc., 1998), pp. 25-26: "Try to bring a person to a decision to 'surrender as much of himself as he knows to as much of God as he knows.' Stay with him until he makes a decision and says it aloud."

Prior to all that, Bill had specifically labeled himself a "conservative atheist."[29] He had also said: "Here again the god of Science—which was then my only god—had well deflated me. I was ready for the message that was soon to come from my alcoholic friend Ebby."[30]

Biblical Names for God They Used

There was much more to the pioneers' knowledge and understanding of our Creator (God Almighty) than present-day AAs are sometimes willing to concede. The words that AAs used in their Big Book (and the words their founders used so frequently) make it abundantly clear that A.A. pioneers understood and knew God as the God described in the Bible, or, as Dr. Bob called it, the *Good Book*. First of all, in the third edition of their Big Book, they used the word "God" a total of at least 277 times, plus specific pronouns referring to God at least 107 times.[31] Then there were the biblical names for God which the Big Book and the early AAs themselves used with some frequency—continuing even to this day. The words were:

- *Creator* [The Bible speaks of God as Creator of the heaven and the earth in Genesis 1:1. It frequently calls God the Creator. Thus Isaiah 40:28 states: "Hast thou not known? hast thou not heard, *that* the everlasting God, the Lord, the Creator of the ends of the earth fainteth not, neither is weary?"[32] A.A.'s Big Book text refers to God as

---

[29]Dick B., *Turning Point: A History of Early A.A.'s Spiritual Roots and Successes* (Kihei, HI: Paradise Research Publications, Inc.), p. 96.

[30]*Three Talks to Medical Societies, supra*, pp. 7-8.

[31]See Dick B., *Turning Point, supra*, p. 158. Also see Stewart C., *A Reference Guide to the Big Book of Alcoholics Anonymous* (Seattle, WA: Recovery Press, Inc., 1986), pp. 115-16.

[32]See also Ecclesiastes 12:1; Isaiah 43:15; Romans 1:25; 1 Peter 4:19.

"Creator" twelve times.[33] Its "Seventh Step Prayer" is addressed to "My Creator."[34] And it takes no semantics scholar to understand that the Creator of the heaven and the earth is not a group, a group of drunks, a lightbulb, a chair, or Santa Claus.]

- *Maker* [The Bible states in Psalm 95:6-7: "O come, let us worship and bow down: let us kneel before the Lord our maker, For he *is* our God. . ." The Big Book twice refers to God as our Maker.[35] And most assuredly it is not speaking of a tree or a stone.]

- *Father* [In his sermon on the mount, Jesus spoke of "your Father which is in heaven;" he addressed the "Lord's prayer" to "Our Father which art in heaven; and he spoke of "he that doeth the will of my Father which is in heaven."[36] Recall: Almost every A.A. meeting concludes with the "Lord's Prayer" and the Big Book speaks of God as "Father."][37]

- *Father of lights* [Seizing upon the name "Father of lights" which the Book of James uses in James 1:17, Bill Wilson referred in the Big Book to God as "Father of Light;" and he also referred to God as "the Father of Lights, who presides over all men."[38] Again, the reference is to God as "Father of lights." *Not to "god, the lightbulb!"*]

- *Spirit* [John 4:24 tells us that God is spirit. And the Big Book so characterizes Him (p. 84).]

---

[33]Big Book pp. 13, 25, 28, 56, 68, 72, 75, 76, 80, 83, 158, 161.

[34]Big Book, p. 76.

[35]Big Book, pp. 57, 63.

[36]Matthew 5:45; 5:48; 6:1; 6:9; 7:11; 7:21.

[37]Big Book, p. 62.

[38]See Dick B., *Turning Point*, p. 159; Big Book, p. 14.

- *Heavenly Father* [See Matthew 63:31; *Alcoholics Anonymous Comes of Age* (New York: Alcoholics Anonymous World Services, Inc., 1957), p. 234; Big Book, p. 181.]

- *The Living God* [See Acts 14:15: "the living God, which made heaven and earth;" Dick B., *The Oxford Group & Alcoholics Anonymous*, 2d ed. (Kihei, HI: Paradise Research Publications, Inc., 1998), pp. 153-155. As shown, Bill Wilson spoke in an earlier manuscript draft of the Big Book of "the way in which he happened to find the living God."]

- *God Almighty* [See Genesis 17:2; 35:11; Exodus 6:3; Ezekiel 10:5. See also Dick B., *The Akron Genesis of Alcoholics Anonymous*, 2d ed., p. 13, for Bill Wilson's use of this term.]

- *God our Father* [See Romans 1:7: ". . . Grace to you and peace from God our Father, and the Lord Jesus Christ." See *Alcoholics Anonymous Comes of Age* (New York: Alcoholics Anonymous World Services, Inc., 1957), p. 105; Dick B., *The Oxford Group & Alcoholics Anonymous*, p. 155].

- *Lord* [See Genesis 17:1: "And when Abram was ninety years old and nine, the Lord appeared to Abram, and said unto him, I *am* the Almighty God; walk before me, and be thou perfect." At page 191 of the Big Book, Bill Wilson and A.A. No. 3 (Bill Dotson) both said "The Lord has been so wonderful to me, curing me of this terrible disease."]

- *God of our fathers* [See 1 Chronicles 12:17; Ezra 7:27; Acts 3:13. At page 29 of *Twelve Steps and Twelve*

Traditions, Bill had written: "The god of intellect displaced the God of our fathers."]

There are endless other references in early A.A. to God, as He is spoken of and described in the Bible. It should be clear from the foregoing specific language that it would test the credibility of a mouse to claim that early A.A., and early AAs and their founders, were speaking of anything other than God Almighty when they used the Biblical expressions quoted above.

Willing Unbelievers Came to Believe in God

John 7:17 and Willingness

There is one unique idea that the Rev. Sam Shoemaker and the Oxford Group imparted to A.A. That is the idea which Shoemaker and the Oxford Group people felt was set forth in John 7:17:

> If any man will do his will, he shall know of the doctrine, whether it be of God, or *whether* I speak of myself.[39]

Long before there was an Oxford Group or a preacher named Sam Shoemaker or a society called Alcoholics Anonymous, the verse in John 7:17 had been used to support the idea that *obedience is the organ of spiritual knowledge.*[40] To the idea of *doing* God's

---

[39]In his second book, Sam Shoemaker began quoting this verse. See Samuel M. Shoemaker, Jr., *A Young Man's View of the Ministry* (New York: Association Press, 1923), p. 41. Sam quoted this verse with great frequency thereafter; and it came to be called Sam's favorite verse. See A. J. Russell, *For Sinner's Only* (London: Hodder and Stoughton Limited, 1932), p. 211.

[40]Henry Drummond, *The Ideal Life: Addresses Hitherto Unpublished* (New York: Hodder & Stoughton, 1897), p. 302. At page 310: "Obedience, as it is sometimes expressed, is the organ of spiritual knowledge. . . . This is one of the great discoveries the Bible has made to the world. It is purely a Bible thought." See also Henry B. Wright, *The Will of God and a Man's Lifework* (New York: Association Press, 1924), pp. 117-30.

will was added the idea of *willingness* to do God's will.[41] And the willingness, they said, came from studying the Bible to determine the universal will of God and waiting quietly and patiently to learn the private or particular will of God. *This meant seeking God's guidance.* And it brought forth a verse which became the watchword for earlier theologians and for Bill's first spiritual teacher, the Rev. Sam Shoemaker. The verse was from Paul's cry to Jesus in the Book of Acts:

> And he [Paul] trembling and astonished said, "Lord, what wilt thou have me to do?" (Acts 9:5).[42]

Obedience and Knowledge

The request to God for instructions and the resultant information was also to be tested by actions consistent with the Four Absolute standards of Jesus—honesty, purity, unselfishness, and love.[43] It meant *doing* the will of God. Oxford Group Founder Dr. Frank N. D. Buchman was well known for the expression:

> God alone can change human nature. The secret lies in that great forgotten truth that when man listens, God speaks; when man obeys, God acts.[44]

Obedience to God's will meant, to Shoemaker, Buchman, and the Oxford Group, checking one's perceived divine guidance against

---

[41]Wright, *The Will of God, supra*, pp. 124-28. At page 126, Wright said: "We therefore revise Robertson's statement to read—Willingness to Do God's Will the Necessary Condition for Knowledge of It."

[42]See Wright, *The Will of God*, p. 144; Samuel M. Shoemaker, Jr., *My Life-Work And My Will* (Pamphlet found in the Episcopal Church Archives, Austin, Texas, in the Shoemaker collection, containing an address given at Concord, New Hampshire, circa January 3-6, 1930), p. 5.

[43]Wright, *The Will of God, supra*, p. 170.

[44]Frank N. D. Buchman, *Remaking the World* (London: Blandford Press, 1961), p. 46.

the Bible and Jesus's principles found in the Four
Absolutes—honesty, purity, unselfishness and love. Pointing out
that sin is the root of unbelief and that the Devil is the author of
the untruth of supposed integrity in sin, Shoemaker rejected
"unbelief about God and life and the goodness of the universe and
the worthwhileness of life."[45] The end result of doing God's will,
said Sam Shoemaker, is finding God and knowing Him. Sam
wrote:

> Knowledge of God is worth more than all the wisdom of the
> world.[46]

There Was A Reward

There was reward for obedience. It was set forth in 1 John 2:17:

> And the world passeth away, and the lust thereof: but he that
> doeth the will of God abideth forever.[47]

The immediate mentor of the Oxford Group, Professor Henry
B. Wright of Yale, expressed the reward as follows:

> Can we even faintly grasp the full meaning of these words, "He
> that doeth the will of God abideth forever"? Abideth how? In
> infinite knowledge, with infinite provisions made for all wants,
> with infinite power to achieve and opportunity for development,
> in everlasting companionship, in perfect freedom, perfect joy,
> perfect peace.[48]

---

[45]Samuel M. Shoemaker, Jr., *Religion That Works* (New York: Fleming H. Revell,
1928), p. 40.

[46]Shoemaker, *Religion That Works*, p. 41.

[47]Wright, *The Will of God, supra*, p. 178.

[48]Wright, *The Will of God, supra*, p. 278.

Action As the Key to Belief

Willingness to try to form a relationship with the Creator became the key and commencing step on the unbeliever's path to a relationship with God and knowledge of God—hence belief.[49] The Big Book promises emphatically:

> Circumstances made him willing to believe. He humbly offered himself to his Maker—then he knew. . . . When we drew near to Him He disclosed Himself to us.[50]

Bill Wilson had concluded from his own experience that if the "god of science" and reliance on things human deflated and defeated the drunk, the drunk would probably turn to the God of the Bible for the simple reason that there was no other power available. He stated:

> Hence if science passed a death sentence on the drunk, and we placed that fearful verdict on our alcoholic transmission belt, one victim talking to another, it might shatter the listener completely. Then the alcoholic might turn to the God of the theologian, there being no other place to go.[51]

The Pioneers Believed That, When Sought, God Heals

Dr. Bob's wife, Anne Ripley Smith, wrote, and frequently shared with early AAs and their families, the contents of the spiritual journal she assembled between 1933 and 1939. She stated unequivocally:

---

[49]Big Book, pp. 12, 13, 25, 28, 47, 57, 58, 59, 60, 67, 69, 70, 76, 79, 93, 124 158.

[50]Big Book, p. 57. Compare James 4:8: "Draw nigh to God, and he will draw nigh to you."

[51]*Three Talks to Medical Societies, supra,* p. 12.

Of course the Bible ought to be the main Source Book of all.
No day ought to pass without reading it. Read until some
passage comes that "hits" you. Then pause and meditate over its
meaning for your life. Begin reading the Bible with the Book of
Acts and follow up with the Gospels and then the Epistles of
Paul. Let "Revelation" alone for a while. The Psalms ought to
be read and the Prophets.[52]

And the Bible *was* regular fare in early A.A. It was read in
individual homes. It was read at the home of Dr. Bob and Anne.
It was read in meetings. And it was the topic of most of the
reading early AAs studied in developing their basic recovery ideas.

Their Bible and God's Healings

The Pioneers' Bibles, and the Bible devotionals they studied, told
them in no uncertain terms that they could be healed by God. The
following are some of the clear verses, with references in footnotes
to literature early AAs read:

- . . . [F]or I *am* the Lord that healeth thee (Exodus 15:26).[53]

- Bless the Lord, O my soul. . . . Who forgiveth all thine
  iniquities; who healeth all thy diseases (Psalm 103:1, 3).[54]

- Then they cry unto the Lord in their trouble, *and* he saveth
  them out of their distresses. He sent his word, and healed
  them . . . (Psalm 107:19-20).[55]

---

[52]See Dick B., *Anne Smith's Journal, supra*, p. 83.

[53]Nora Smith Holm, *The Runner's Bible* (New York: Houghton Mifflin Company,
1915), p. 107.

[54]Holm, *The Runner's Bible*, p. 109; Glenn Clark, *I Will Lift Up Mine Eyes* (New
York: Harper & Brothers, 1937), p. 147; Harry Emerson Fosdick, *The Meaning of Faith*
(New York: The Abingdon Press, 1917), pp. 53-54.

[55]Holm, *The Runner's Bible*, p. 110.

- . . . Thus saith the Lord, the God of David thy father, I have heard thy prayer. I have seen thy tears; behold, I will heal thee . . . (2 Kings 20:5).[56]

- I have seen his ways, and will heal him (Isaiah 57:18).[57]

- For I will restore health unto thee, and I will heal thee of thy wounds, saith the Lord (Jeremiah 30:17).[58]

- Behold, I will bring it health and cure, and I will cure them, and will reveal unto them the abundance of peace and truth (Jeremiah 33:6).[59]

- According to your faith be it unto you (Matthew 9:28).[60]

- The blind receive their sight, and the lame walk, the lepers are cleansed, and the deaf hear, the dead are raised up, and the poor have the gospel preached to them (Matthew 11:5).[61]

- Again I say unto you, That if two of you shall agree on earth as touching anything that they shall ask, it shall be done for them of my Father which is in heaven. For where two or three are gathered together in my name, there am I in the midst of them (Matthew 18:19-20).[62]

---

[56]Holm, *The Runner's Bible*, p. 114.

[57]Holm, *The Runner's Bible*, p. 114.

[58]Holm, *The Runner's Bible*, p. 109; Clark, *I Will Lift Up Mine Eyes*, p. 147.

[59]Holm, *The Runner's Bible*, p. 110.

[60]Holm, *The Runner's Bible*, p. 114.

[61]Holm, *The Runner's Bible*, p. 119.

[62]Holm, *The Runner's Bible*, pp. 64-65. E. Stanley Jones, *Victorious Living* (New York: The Abingdon Press, 1936), p. 251; Clark, *I Will Lift Up Mine Eyes*, p. 24; Harry Emerson Fosdick, *The Meaning of Prayer* (New York: Association Press, 1934), pp. 124, 178.

- And Jesus said unto him, Go thy way; thy faith hath made thee whole. And immediately he received his sight, and followed Jesus in the way (Mark 10:52).[63]

- Verily, verily, I say unto you, He that believeth on me, the works that I do shall he do also; and greater *works* than these shall he do; because I go unto my Father (John 14:12).[64]

- And whatsoever ye shall ask in my name, that will I do, that the Father may be glorified in the Son. If ye shall ask anything in my name, I will do it (John 14:13-14).[65]

- And his name through faith in his name hath made this man strong whom ye see and know: yea, the faith which is by him hath given him perfect soundness in the presence of you all (Acts 3:16).[66]

- And the prayer of faith shall save the sick, and the Lord shall raise him up; and if he shall have committed sins, they shall be forgiven him. Confess your faults one to another, and pray for one another, that ye may be healed. The effectual fervent prayer of a righteous man availeth much (James 5:15-16).[67]

- And this is the confidence that we have in him, that, if we ask anything according to his will, he heareth us: And if we

---

[63]Holm, *The Runner's Bible*, p. 114.

[64]Holm, *The Runner's Bible*, p. 123; Glenn Clark, *The Soul's Sincere Desire* (Boston: Little, Brown, and Company, 1927), p. 18; Oswald Chambers, *My Utmost for His Highest* (New Jersey: Barbour and Company, Inc., 1935), p. 291; *The Upper Room* for October 2, 1935.

[65]Holm, *The Runner's Bible*, p. 64; Chambers, *My Utmost for His Highest*, p. 159; *The Upper Room* for July 28, 1937; Clark, *I Will Lift Up Mine Eyes*, pp. 18, 114; Fosdick, *The Meaning of Prayer*, p. 129.

[66]Holm, *The Runner's Bible*, p. 114.

[67]Jones, *Victorious Living*, p. 204; Holm, *The Runner's Bible*, p. 114. *The Upper Room* for August 19, 1935; December 4, 1935; Fosdick, *The Meaning of Prayer*, pp. 157-58.

know that he hear us, whatsoever we ask, we know that we
have the petitions that we desired of him (1 John 5:14-15).[68]

Bill W.'s Inaccurate and Incomplete Description of A.A. Sources

In some of his less explicit, less accurate, and less generous
moments, Bill Wilson attributed almost every A.A. idea to four
basic sources. Noticeably, he neglected to mention God, the Bible,
Jesus Christ, Anne Smith (Dr. Bob's wife), and Christian literature
early AAs studied. In so doing, Bill may have set the stage for the
demise of A.A.'s early belief in God and that God *cures* and heals.

Bill, more than once, led others to believe his Twelve Steps
were culled from what he had been taught by Dr. William Duncan
Silkworth of Towns Hospital, by his reading of the work of "the
famed psychologist William James, called by some the father of
modern psychology," by the teachings of the Rev. Sam Shoemaker
and the Oxford Group, and from the vital advice from Dr. Carl
Gustav Jung of Switzerland that a conversion experience was
needed.[69]

The alleged founders or founding elements, according to Bill's
flawed and incomplete reconstruction of the roots, were: (1) Dr.
William Duncan Silkworth (who told Bill about the disease and its
seeming hopelessness without a psychic change); (2) Dr. Carl
Gustav Jung (who told Bill's mentor Rowland Hazard that a
conversion experience would be necessary for his cure and might
be achieved through religious sources). (3) The writings of
Professor William James in *The Varieties of Religious Experience*
(who supposedly validated for Bill the reality of Bill's "hot flash"
experience in Towns Hospital where Bill recovered and never
again doubted the existence of God). (4) The Rev. Sam Shoemaker

---

[68]Holm, *The Runner's Bible*, p. 65; Clark, *I Will Lift Up Mine Eyes*, pp. 19, 24.

[69]See *Pass It On*, pp. 114, 123-31, 169, 171, 174, 196-99, 381-87; *The Language of the Heart: Bill W.'s Grapevine Writings* (New York: The AA Grapevine, Inc., 1988), pp. 195-96, 296-98, 379-80.

(whom Bill crowned with the wreath of "co-founder" and who had, *according to Bill only*, taught Bill every one of the spiritual principles of the Twelve Steps, except possibly those in Step One and Step Twelve).[70]

Yet Bill had gathered together, as the alleged A.A. sources, a polyglot group, as far as belief in God's healing power was concerned. Therefore, let us examine briefly each of the four influences Bill cited:

- *First, Towns Hospital Director and Psychiatrist William Duncan Silkworth, M.D.*: Little known is the fact that *Dr. Silkworth strongly believed in the healing power of Jesus* Christ—particularly in the alcoholism field where Silkworth was a renowned expert.[71]

- *Second, The Oxford Group and the Rev. Sam Shoemaker*: The Oxford Group sobered up a good many drunks by bringing them to Christ before A.A. was founded, but that was not the particular focus of its founder Dr. Frank Buchman. On the other hand, the Rev. Sam Shoemaker was the active agent in bringing Russell Firestone of Akron to Christ and Firestone's consequent miraculous, albeit somewhat short-lived, deliverance from alcoholism.[72] Sam certainly worked with other drunks to help them get healed of alcoholism.[73] And Sam was the enthusiastic rector of Calvary Church which achieved unique and great results

---

[70]The author has emphasized "Bill only" because Dr. Bob was very explicit in his statement that the basic ideas of A.A. came from the pioneers' study of the Bible. *DR. BOB*, p. 97.

[71]See the extended account in Norman Vincent Peale, *The Positive Power of Jesus Christ: Life-changing Adventures in Faith* (New York: Foundation For Christian Living, 1980), pp. 59-63.

[72]See account in Dick B., *The Akron Genesis of Alcoholics Anonymous*, 2d ed., pp. 17-51.

[73]Bill Pittman and Dick B., *Courage to Change: The Christian Roots of the Twelve-Step Movement* (Center City, MN: Hazelden, 1998), pp. 135-50.

with drunks, including Bill Wilson and Bill's sponsor Ebby Thacher, at its Calvary Rescue Mission. A. J. Russell told part of the story in *For Sinners Only*:

> "One evening at Calvary I saw an astonishing sight for an Episcopalian church. Calvary had a rescue mission run by a remarkable superintendent named Harry Hadley. That evening Harry had brought up with him a hundred or two men rescued by the mission from the streets of New York. Instead of a sermon these men were invited to stand in their pews and tell what contact with Christ had meant to them. If ever one was conscious of the Holy Spirit in a church service it was at that extraordinary evensong. There was no waiting. Men popped up one after the other from all points of the front rows of pews and rattled out their life-stories. The pathetic tales they told of broken homes mended, of drunkenness cured, of victory over vice, of the new reign of love in lives and homes previously disordered, divided, discordant, would have melted the heart of the most complacent modern Pharisee. And at the end the invitation was given to others to come forward to the altar and dedicate their lives to the service of Christ, the Mender of men. Most unique of all—there were responses. In an Episcopalian Church" (pp. 213-14).

On the other hand, Shoemaker's had an immense interest "standing by the door" and encouraging atheists and agnostics to *find* God.[74] Unfortunately, in a number of important ways, this has left Sam Shoemaker (who was, and could have continued to be, counted as a major spokesman for the healing power of God Almighty) with a legacy that emphasizes Sam's "act as if" ideas.[75] It has

---

[74]S. M. Shoemaker, *So I Stand by the Door and Other Verses* (Pittsburgh, PA: Calvary Rectory, 1958), pp. 5-6.

[75]See, for example, Samuel M. Shoemaker, "Act As If," *Christian Herald*, October, 1954.

meant, so far as A.A. recognition and appreciation are concerned, that Sam may be remembered far more for his "experiment of faith" than for his role as Bible Christian, voluminous Christian writer, teacher of Christian ideas, pastor, priest, and churchman in the Protestant Episcopal Church—the man who really brought Bill Wilson to a belief in God and in Jesus Christ as Savior.[76]

- *Third, Psychiatrist Dr. Carl Gustav Jung*: Dr. Carl Jung's beliefs about the power of God—the God of the Bible—are *difficult to discern*. In his book, *Modern Man in Search of a Soul* (which both Bill and Dr. Bob apparently read), Jung said:

> I should like to call attention to the following facts. During the past thirty years, people from all the civilized countries of the earth have consulted me. I have treated many hundreds of patients, the larger number being Protestants, a smaller number Jews, and not more than five or six believing [Roman] Catholics. Among all my patients in the second half of life—that is to say, over thirty-five—there has not been one whose problem in the last resort was not that of finding a *religious outlook on life*. It is safe to say that every one of them fell ill because he had lost that which the living religions of every age have given to their followers, and none of them has really been healed who did not regain his religious outlook. This of course has nothing whatever to do with a particular creed or membership of a church.[77]

Note that Jung hardly passes specific bouquets to Christian believers, Christian denominations, or Christian churches.

---

[76]See extended discussion in Dick B., *New Light on Alcoholism: God, Sam Shoemaker, and A.A.* (Kihei, HI: Paradise Research Publications, Inc., 1999).

[77]C.G. Jung, *Modern Man in Search of a Soul* (New York: Harcourt Brace Jovanovich, Publishers, 1933), p. 229 (emphasis added).

Note also that Jung speaks of a "religious outlook" rather than belief in the Lord Jesus Christ, which was an essential in early A.A. Jung certainly does speak of "healing" but seems to be talking with reference to his own practice, which presumably involved primarily mental difficulties. And he concludes with a somewhat platitudinous compliment to *all* kinds of religions.

- *Finally, Psychology Professor William James of Harvard*: William James was long dead by the time A.A. was founded. Yet he was called an A.A. "founder" by Bill Wilson. And Professor James occupies a prominent, but confusing place in A.A. history. In many ways, *William James could be called an "author of confusion"*—a great amount of confusion occurring in A.A. language.[78]

First of all, Bill Wilson was supposed to have read William James's book *The Varieties of Religious Experience* while Wilson was still a patient at Towns Hospital, barely sober, and therefore presumably still detoxing.[79] Second, some historians have stated that Wilson validated his Towns Hospital "religious experience" as a result of what he learned from James's book.[80] Yet others have questioned whether Bill might in fact have simply been experiencing hallucinations during his "hot flash" experience.[81] Others have concluded that Wilson really thought he had perceived in James's book a necessary principle for recovery—deflation-at-

---

[78]Compare 1 Corinthians 14:33: "For God is not *the author* of confusion, but of peace, as in all churches of the saints."

[79]See *Pass It On*, pp. 124-25. Also, see Dick B. *Turning Point*, p. 98, for citations to other discussions of this point. For James' title, see William James, *The Varieties of Religious Experience: A Study in Human Nature* (New York: Vintage Books: The Library of America, 1990).

[80]See Bill Pittman, *AA The Way It Began* (Seattle, WA: Glen Abbey Books, 1988), p. 154.

[81]Mel B., *New Wine: The Spiritual Roots of the Twelve Step Miracle* (Center City, MN: Hazelden, 1991), p. 77

depth.[82] Yet one historian claims that neither the phrase "deflation-at-depth" nor the bare word *deflation* appears anywhere in James's *Varieties*.[83] To make matters still more confusing—even though James was neither clergyman nor theologian—his work was favorably cited or read by almost every conceivable A.A. source that contributed either to the Oxford Group *or* A.A.'s founding.[84]

A.A.'s Christian Fellowship, as it was called in the 1930's, and its Christian mentors and founders were working to bringing alcoholics to Jesus Christ, recovery, and deliverance.[85] Typical confirmations of this fact are the following remarks:

- *Ed A., oldtimer from Lorain, Ohio*: "They would not let you in unless you surrendered to Jesus Christ on your knees."[86]

---

[82]Pittman, *AA The Way It Began*, p. 154.

[83]Ernest Kurtz, *Not-God: A History of Alcoholics Anonymous*, Exp. ed. (Center City, MN: Hazelden, 1991), p. 23.

[84]Harold Begbie, *Twice-Born Men* (New York: Fleming H. Revell, 1909), pp. 16-17; *Life Changers* (London: Mills & Boon Limited, 1923), pp. 32, 139; H.A. Walter, *Soul Surgery: Some Thoughts on Incisive Personal Work*, 6th ed. (London: Blandford Press, n.d.), pp. 78-86; Mel B., *Ebby: The Man Who Sponsored Bill W.* (Center City, MN: Hazelden, 1998), p. 70; Samuel M. Shoemaker, Jr., *Realizing Religion* (New York: Association Press, 1923), pp. vii, 4, 22, 26, 35, 62; Dick B., *Anne Smith's Journal, 1933-1939: A.A.'s Principles of Success*, 3rd ed. (Kihei, HI: Paradise Research Publications, Inc., 1998), pp. 27-28, 64-65, 68, 103; *Dr. Bob and His Library: A Major A.A. Spiritual Source*, 3rd ed. (Kihei: HI: Paradise Research Publications, Inc., 1998), pp. 54-55; *The Books Early AAs Read for Spiritual Growth*, 7th ed. (Kihei, HI: Paradise Research Publications, Inc., 1998), pp. 59, 62.

[85]Dick B., *The Akron Genesis of Alcoholics Anonymous*, 2d ed., pp. 192-97; *That Amazing Grace*, pp. 27-28; Charles Clapp, Jr., *The Big Bender* (New York: Harper & Brothers Publishers, 1938), pp. 106-09, 112-14, 126-28; Clarence Snyder, *Going Through The Steps* (Altamonte Springs, FL: Stephen Foreman, 1985); *DR. BOB and the Good Oldtimers*, p. 118.

[86]Recorded telephone conversation with Danny W. in Lancaster, California, from Lorain, Ohio, on January 9, 1994, in which Ed A. made that statement.

- *Larry B., oldtimer from Cleveland, Ohio*: "They took me upstairs to be a born again human being and be God's helper to alcoholics."[87]

- *Clarence S., Dr. Bob's sponsee, who got sober February 11, 1938*: Clarence said that he went upstairs to T. Henry Williams's master bedroom with Dr. Bob, T. Henry Williams, and an Oxford Group member. These men told Clarence to get on his knees, and they joined him on their knees around T. Henry's bed. These three men then led Clarence through a "Sinner's Prayer." Clarence said the prayer was the very one Dr. Bob had used from the beginning of A.A. surrenders in Akron.[88]

These surrenders to Jesus Christ occurred despite the fact that Bill's mentor, William James, had written about an "higher power," "higher powers," "the experience of exteriority of the helping power," "a personal god or gods," "harmonious relation with that higher universe," and "prayer or inner communion with the spirit thereof—be that spirit 'God' or 'law,'" and that "being the instrument of a higher power is of course 'inspiration.'"[89]

Such comments were based on James's apparent unwillingness to differentiate between: (1) "the whole range of Christian saints and heresiarchs, including the greatest, the Bernards, the Loyolas, the Luthers, the Foxes, the Wesleys" [and] (2) "the teachings of the Buddha, of Jesus, of Saint Paul (apart from his gift of tongues), of Saint Augustine, of Huss, of Luther, of Wesley."[90] The self-styled conservative atheist Bill Wilson belonged to no church, had never studied the Bible until he lived with Dr. Bob and his wife in Akron, and was then or later hearing ideas from

---

[87]Letter from Larry B. to the author, dated September 18, 1992, in which Larry B. stated he was in and out of the A.A. fellowship between 1939 and 1944. He stated that his own surrender was as described in the quote.

[88]See extended discussion in Dick B., *Turning Point*, pp. 140-42.

[89]James, *The Varieties of Religious Experience*, pp. 224, 429, 435, 454-56.

[90]James, *The Varieties of Religious Experience*, pp. 428-29

the likes of Mary Baker Eddy, Aldous Huxley, Gerald Heard, Emmet Fox, the Rev. Sam Shoemaker, Father Ed Dowling, and Monsignor Fulton J. Sheen.

Is it any wonder that Bill should opt for, and enlarge upon some amorphous and ill-defined "power." This was a "power" which—before long—came to be the "something" or the "nothing at all" that today's A.A. has made it. In fact, at several levels, A.A. continues to promote that weird "power" idea quite frequently today—to the point of making it doctrinal.[91]

Strangely, A.A.'s *Came to Believe* contains a wealth of stories by AAs who chose their own conception of *God*. Yet its introduction to Chapter 8, titled "A Higher Power," contains the following quote from Bill Wilson, apparently written for the A.A. *Grapevine* in 1961, some ten years after Dr. Bob was dead:

> Our concepts of a Higher Power and God—as we understand Him—afford everyone a nearly unlimited choice of spiritual belief and action (*Came to Believe*, p. 77).

In the author's view, this statement is reflective of A.A. as it exists today and is definitely doctrinal. By doctrinal is meant that this is the format for A.A. publications and chatter. It does not represent the views of AAs as they marched to victory over alcoholism through the help of God Almighty between 1935 and 1939.

Bill's Own Writings Continued the Original Emphasis on God

We return to the proposition that Bill basically stuck to the biblical principles he learned in Akron, was taught by Sam Shoemaker, and heard frequently at his Oxford Group meetings in the Midwest and in the New York area. Bill never really stopped talking about

---

[91]See the A.A. pamphlets previously quoted and the *Daily Reflections* book of A.A. See also *Came to Believe* (New York: Alcoholics Anonymous World Services, Inc., 1973), pp. 80, 83, 86, 114, 116.

God Almighty in each edition of his Big Book, in his own writings, and in his addresses to AAs and others. For example, in Bill's lecture at the Yale Summer School of Alcohol Studies in 1944, Bill used the following expressions:[92]

- Ebby said, "Where does religion come in?" . . . his [Oxford Group] friends went on to say, "Ebby, it is our experience that no one can carry out such a program with enough thoroughness and enough continuity on pure self-sufficiency. One must have help. . . . So, call on God as you understand God. Try prayer" (p. 463).[93]

- That experience led us to examine some of the obscure phrases that we sometimes see in our Bibles. For a great many of us have taken to reading the Bible (p. 467).[94]

- [Of Jimmy Burwell] It was his prideful obstinacy. He had thought to himself, "Maybe thee fellows have something with their God-business." His hand reached out, in the darkness, and touched something on his bureau. It was a Gideon Bible. Jimmy picked it up and he read from it. I do not know just what he read, and I have always had a queer reluctance to ask him. But Jimmy has not had a drink to this day, and that was about 5 years ago (p. 468).[95]

---

[92]*Lecture 29, The Fellowship of Alcoholics Anonymous by W.W.*, Twenty-nine Lectures with Discussions as given at the Yale Summer School of Alcohol Studies (New Haven: Quarterly Journal of Studies on Alcohol, 1945).

[93]2 Corinthians 3:4-5: "And such trust have we through Christ to God-ward: Not that we are sufficient of ourselves to think any thing as of ourselves; but our sufficiency *is* of God."

[94]2 Timothy 2:15: "Study to shew thyself approved unto God, a workman that needeth not to be ashamed, rightly dividing the word of truth."

[95]John 5:39: "Search the scriptures; for in them ye think ye have eternal life: and they are they which testify of me." Acts 17:11-12: "These were more noble than those in Thessalonica, in that they received the word with all readiness of mind, and searched the scriptures daily, whether those things were so. Therefore many of them believed; also of honorable women which were Greeks, and of men, not a few."

- Indeed, "What hath God wrought!" (p. 470).[96]

Bill's friend and original spiritual teacher Sam Shoemaker was invited to attend and did attend an annual A.A. dinner celebrating Bill Wilson's 20th Anniversary. It was held on Tuesday, November 9, 1954, at the Grand Ballroom of the Commodore Hotel. Sam took copious notes which the author found in the Episcopal Church Archives in Texas. Sam noted:

> "Who invented AA?" says Bill. "It was God Almighty that invented AA. This is the story of how we learned to be free. God grant that AA and the program of recovery and unity and service be a story that continues into the future as long as God needs it."[97]

And all of Bill's writings were liberally salted with references to the Creator, Father, Almighty God, Maker, living God, God of our Fathers, and Father of lights (Whose characteristics Bill Wilson fully understood and fully intended to convey when he spoke. He even intended this when he wrote into his much-contested Twelve Traditions, of a "loving God as He may express Himself in our Group Conscience.")[98]

Bill's Revealing Remarks to Father John C. Ford, S.J.

Bill wrote, in May, 1957, to Father John Cuthbert Ford, S.J., who had edited one, and was editing the second of, Bill's important

---

[96]Mark 6:2-3: "And when the sabbath day was come, he [Jesus] began to teach in the synagogue: and many hearing *him* were astonished, saying from whence hath this *man* these things? and what wisdom *is* this which is given unto him, that even such mighty works are wrought by his hands? Is not this the carpenter, the son of Mary. . . ."

[97]Record Group 101, Box 23, Folder 59, Archives of the Episcopal Church.

[98]Big Book, p. 564; 1 John 4:8, 16 ["God is love."].

A.A. publications (*Alcoholics Anonymous Comes of Age* and *Twelve Steps and Twelve Traditions*[99]):

> You will remember there was another spot in the manuscript where the Buddhists wanted to substitute the word "Good" for "God" in the Twelve Steps. Here I felt I could make only a partial accommodation. To begin with, the Steps are not enforceable upon anyone—they are only suggestions. A belief in the Steps or in God is not in any way a requisite for A.A. membership. Therefore we have no means of compelling anyone to stay away from A.A. because he does not believe in God or the Twelve Steps. In fact, A.A. has a technique of reducing rebellion among doubting people by deliberately inviting them to disagree with everything we believe in. We merely suggest that the doubters stick around and get acquainted. They are assured they are members if they say so. In truth, many an agnostic or atheist newcomer, including some fallen away [Roman] Catholics, have substituted the word "Good" for "God" in the Twelve Steps. By practicing the program with "Good" in mind, they almost invariably come back to some kind of a concept of God—usually a personal God. Whether this will happen to our Buddhist members, I don't know. *But it certainly can't make the least difference to any of us what the Buddhists do with the Steps.*[100]

Bill's Alleged Four A.A. Sources Revisited

Let's look again at the four alleged sources of A.A. ideas that Bill Wilson cited.

---

[99]See Ford's statement corroborating this fact on July 31, 1998, in his Foreword to Mary C. Darrah, *Sister Ignatia: Angel of Alcoholics Anonymous* (Chicago: Loyola University Press, 1992), p. x.

[100]Letter from Wilson to Ford, dated May 14, 1957, Archives of the Episcopal Church, Record Group 101, Box 30, Folder—Wilson having forwarded to Sam Shoemaker copies of his correspondence with Father Ford when Ford was editing *A.A. Comes of Age* and *Twelve Steps and Traditions* in the 1950's (emphasis added).

First, Dr. Silkworth: **Dr. William D. Silkworth believed** God could *heal* the alcoholic when the alcoholic surrendered his entire self to Jesus Christ.[101]

Second, Dr. Jung: Unknowingly, as far his expectation of any later impact on A.A. is concerned, **Dr. Carl Jung was waffling** between the importance of "religious outlook" in healing the mind, and yet conceding to Rowland Hazard in 1931 that the chronic alcoholic could only be healed by a conversion experience.[102] In fact, Bill quoted Dr. Jung's comments to Rowland Hazard as follows:

> Ordinary religious faith isn't enough. What I'm talking about is a transforming experience, a conversion experience, if you like.
> . . . The lightning of the transforming experience of conversion may then strike you. This you must try—it is your only way out.[103]

Third, Rev. Shoemaker: **The Rev. Sam Shoemaker not only believed in the efficacy of God's healing; he helped alcoholics to that healing and wrote specifically about helping the physically sick and the mentally sick.**[104]

Fourth, Professor James: Professor William James seemed to validate the healing of alcoholics through "religious experiences." He discussed prayers for the recovery of sick people and said it should be encouraged as a therapeutic measure.[105] But **Professor James mixes up prayer and miraculous healings with talk of mysticism; transcendentalism; absorption of spiritual power or**

---

[101]Peale, *The Positive Power of Jesus Christ, supra*, p. 60.

[102]Jung, *Modern Man in Search of a Soul*, p. 229; *Pass It On*, pp. 381-386.

[103]*Three Talks to Medical Societies, supra*, p. 7.

[104]Samuel M. Shoemaker, Jr., *How You Can Help Other People* (New York: E. P. Dutton & Co., Inc., 1946), pp. 118-47.

[105]James, *The Varieties of Religious Experience*, p. 415.

grace; "higher powers;" "God;" "law;" supernaturalism; suggestion; "hystero-demonopathy;" Stoic conduct; sudden raptures; faith-state; prayer-state; the "more" and the meaning of our "union" with it; and other ideas.[106]

It should be acknowledged, of course that James was writing as a psychologist. James therefore may have been well within the appropriate province of his discussion; but his treatise hardly sheds much light on the spiritual concepts of the Bible, the power of God, or the miracles performed by God, by Jesus Christ, by the Apostles, and by other believers then and now. In fact, when James endeavored to analyze "higher power," he may have set the stage for Bill's confusion and A.A.'s present literature.[107]

As the author looked at such remarks by William James, he was compelled to wish that James, Shoemaker, Wilson, and later A.A. had given more thought to the significance of the following statement by Jesus Christ:

> Jesus answered and said unto him, Ye do err, not knowing the scriptures, nor the power of God (Matthew 22:29).

In this respect, the words in Daniel are also appropriate, perhaps as to James's prayer discussion and Bill Wilson's interpretation of it:

> TEKEL: Thou art weighed in the balances, and art found wanting (Daniel 5:27).

---

[106]James, *The Varieties of Religious Experience*, pp. 415-63.

[107]Again, see James, *The Varieties of Religious Experience*, *supra*, p. 224: "If there be higher powers able to impress us, they may get access to us only through the subliminal door;" p. 454: "The solution is a sense that *we are saved from the wrongness* by making proper connection with the higher powers;" p. 429: "The great field for this sense of being the instrument of a higher power is of course 'inspiration'."

As we will see shortly, Bill Wilson himself plainly expressed his belief that God could *cure* alcoholism and that the healing needed to arise from *conversion*.

3

Their Path, Jesus Christ, and a Relationship with God

The author has written a number of titles on the spiritual roots of Alcoholics Anonymous. The research for these titles confirms that the basic sources of A.A.'s spiritual ideas are six in number: (1) The Bible.[1] (2) Quiet Time and the Bible devotionals.[2] (3) The teachings of the Rev. Sam Shoemaker.[3] (4) The life-changing program of the Oxford Group.[4] (5) The contents of Anne Smith's Journal.[5] (6) The Christian literature the pioneers read.[6] We will not here detail either the sources or the principles. But they all add up to the A.A. conception that certain spiritual steps, adapted

---

[1] Dick B., *The Good Book and The Big Book: A.A.'s Roots in the Bible*, 2d ed. (Kihei, HI: Paradise Research Publications, Inc., 1997).

[2] Dick B., *Good Morning!: Quiet Time, Morning Watch, Meditation, and Early A.A.*, 2d ed. (Kihei, HI: Paradise Research Publications, Inc., 1998).

[3] Dick B., *New Light on Alcoholism: God, Sam Shoemaker, and A.A.* (Kihei, HI: Paradise Research Publications, Inc., 1999).

[4] Dick B., *The Oxford Group & Alcoholics Anonymous: A Design for Living That Works*, 2d ed. (Kihei, HI: Paradise Research Publications, Inc., 1998).

[5] Dick B., *Anne Smith's Journal, 1933-1939: A.A.'s Principles of Success*, 3rd ed. (Kihei, HI: Paradise Research Publications, Inc., 1998).

[6] Dick B., *Dr. Bob and His Library: A Major A.A. Spiritual Source*, 3rd ed. (Kihei, HI: Paradise Research Publications, Inc., 1998); *The Books Early AAs Read for Spiritual Growth*, 7th ed. (Kihei, HI: Paradise Research Publications, Inc., 1998).

primarily from the Oxford Group's biblical ideas, need to be taken
to have a conversion, a healing, and a relationship with God.

Steps Along the Path

The steps the Oxford Group progenitors of A.A. followed along
the path, and their Twelve Step counterparts themselves, are as
follows:

- **Admission of an unmanageable life (Step One).**

- **Belief or willingness to believe in God (Step Two).**

- **Decision to surrender one's life to God's care (Step Three).**

- **Inventory of blocks keeping one from God (Step Four).**

- **Confession of transgressions (Step Five).**

- **Conviction as to error of one's ways and need to change (Step Six).**

- **Conversion to Christ and resultant relationship with God as His children (Step Seven).**

- **Restitution for harms and restoration of human relationships (Steps Eight and Nine).**

- **Continuance of life-changing practices thus learned (Step Ten).**

- **Continued reliance upon God for truth, guidance, love, and help (Step Eleven).**

The Miraculous Result

We are speaking here about the result AAs obtained from taking the path to a relationship with God. In fact, we are talking about A.A.'s Twelfth Step. As to that Twelfth Step along the early AAs' the path to a relationship with God, there were and are three basic ideas: (1) That the taking of the previous steps produced a spiritual result. (2) That those who obtained the result were to pass along to others the message of what they had done. (3) That the Steps produced a life-change which would become of importance only if it was evidenced in the walk of those who claimed to have become empowered by their new relationship with God.

How They Expressed the Result

Early on, Dr. Frank N.D. Buchman—the Oxford Group founder who really laid out the life-changing steps—provided a simple formula which described the problem, the power, *and* the result. He called the "three essential factors" involved in conversion: *Sin, Jesus Christ*, and *a Miracle*.[7] Buchman's formula was set forth in Howard Walter's *Soul Surgery* with references to William James's *The Varieties of Religious Experience*, Professor Starbuck's *Psychology of Religion* (a work much discussed by James), and Professor Royce's *The Philosophy of Loyalty* (Royce being one of James's Harvard colleagues).[8] The formula was followed by references to conversion and the transformations of drunks described in Finney's *Memoirs*, S. H. Hadley's *Down in Water Street*, and Harold Begbie's *Twice Born Men*.[9] And also by reference to the miraculous healing of the man lame from birth who was told by Peter and John, as related in Acts 3:1-8, "In the

---

[7]H. A. Walter, *Soul Surgery: Some Thoughts on Incisive Personal Work*, 6th ed (London: Blandford Press, n.d.), p. 86. This work, quoting Buchman who helped to write it, was copyrighted in 1919.

[8]Walter, *Soul Surgery*, pp. 78-82.

[9]Walter, *Soul Surgery*, pp. 83-86.

name of Jesus Christ of Nazareth, rise up and walk."[10] In other
words, *A.A.'s spiritual mentors* (in the Oxford Group and among
the Oxford Group's progenitors) *expected miracles*, even with
respect to alcoholics. Reformulated by Buchman's followers in
later years, the three Bible factors involved in mankind's rebellion
against God, his decision to accept Jesus Christ as the redeemer,
and the miracles that flow out of the decision to cooperate with
God were: *Sin—the disease; Christ—the cure; the result—a
miracle.*[11]

One of Sam Shoemaker's earlier books quoted William James
on self-surrender. At a later point, it related stories of those whose
lives had been changed by accepting Christ. But it began by
introducing the whole subject as follows:

> We believe entirely that conversion is the experience which
> initiates the new life. But we are not fools enough to think that
> the beginning is the end! All subsequent life is a development
> of the relationship with God which conversion opened. . . . I
> only hope [said Sam Shoemaker] that these stories breathe life,
> and make religion seem alive and attractive and workable. All
> of us who have had part in writing them will be well enough
> rewarded if only a few are helped towards Christ by what we
> have written.[12]

There is no need to detail materials covered in our other titles as
to the many names used by the Oxford Group, by Shoemaker, and
by AAs themselves to describe the end result of a transformed life.
But the names given to the result included: An experience of God,
a vital experience of Jesus Christ, a religious experience, a
spiritual experience, a spiritual awakening, a relationship with

---

[10]Walter, *Soul Surgery*, p. 86.

[11]*Foundations for Faith*, 2d ed., compiled by Harry Almond (London: Grosvenor, 1980), pp. 9-29.

[12]Samuel M. Shoemaker, Jr., *Children of the Second Birth: Being a Narrative of Spiritual Miracles in a City Parish* (New York: Fleming H. Revell Company, 1927), p. 16.

God, a sense of the power and presence of God, finding God, being in touch with God, contact with God, conversion, surrender, change, being born again, and God-consciousness.[13] And you will find these, or similar, expressions throughout A.A.'s literature.[14]

The Message They Formulated and Preached

The author has heard all kinds of comments within the rooms of A.A. as to what the A.A. message *is*. Yet the essence of the message was and is simple. It did not really change from the days of Jesus Christ and the Apostles, to the Oxford Group days, to A.A.'s own beginnings. It can even be found in the "Golden Text" set forth in A.A.'s Big Book, at page 191, today—which will be discussed in a moment. But that real message seems to have been relegated to the back burner.

In the Bible, it was as follows: John had heard in prison the works of Christ. John sent disciples to ask if Jesus was the one that was to come or whether to look for another. Jesus gave this message to the disciples:

> Go and shew John again those things which ye do hear and see: The blind receive their sight, and the lame walk, the lepers are cleansed, and the deaf hear, the dead are raised up, and the poor have the gospel preached to them (Matthew 11:4-5).

---

[13]Dick B., *The Oxford Group & Alcoholics Anonymous: A Design for Living that Works*, 2d ed. (Kihei, HI: Paradise Research Publications, Inc., 1998), pp. 275-85.

[14]Big Book, 3rd ed.: religious experience, p. 28; spiritual experience, p. 25; spiritual awakening, p. 60; relationship with God, p. 29; consciousness of the presence of God, p. 51; finding God, p. 59; contact with God, 59; change, p. 569; born again, p. 63, God consciousness, p. 570. References to surrender and conversion can readily be found in other A.A. "Conference Approved" literature containing stories of Akron A.A. and stories of Bill Wilson's correspondence with Dr. Carl Jung.

Go and tell the miracles you have seen, said Jesus. When Peter
and John brought about the healing of the impotent man at the
temple gate, they were questioned concerning by what power, or
by what name, they had done this. And Peter replied:

> If we this day be examined of the good deed done to the
> impotent man, by what means he is made whole; Be it known
> unto you all, and to all the people of Israel, that by the name of
> Jesus Christ of Nazareth, whom ye crucified, whom God raised
> from the dead, *even* by him doth this man stand before you
> whole. . . . Neither is there salvation in any other: for there is
> none other name under heaven given among men, whereby we
> must be saved. Now when they saw the boldness of Peter and
> John, and perceived that they were ignorant men, they
> marveled; and they took knowledge of them, that they had been
> with Jesus. And beholding the man which was healed standing
> with them, they could say nothing against it (Acts 4:9-13).

In Sam Shoemaker's teachings, the foregoing examples were
used to guide Sam's followers in witnessing. Share what you have
seen and experienced, Sam said. Give them "news, not views," he
emphasized; for, said he, "The Gospel was originally "news," not
views."[15]

And early AAs picked up on this same theme: They shared
stories of what they had done, not what they thought. They used
the phrase "news, not views."[16] And *their news*—over and over
again—was illustrated by the following Big Book language:

> But my friend [Ebby Thacher] sat before me [Bill Wilson], and
> he made the point-blank declaration that God had done for him
> what he could not do for himself (Big Book, p. 11).

---

[15]Samuel M. Shoemaker, Jr., *The Conversion of the Church* (New York: Fleming H.
Revell Company, 1932), p. 73.

[16]*DR. BOB and the Good Oldtimers* (New York: Alcoholics Anonymous World
Services, Inc., 1980), p. 55; Dick B., *The Akron Genesis of Alcoholics Anonymous*, 2d
ed., pp. 99, 237-38.

We shall tell you what we have done (Big Book, p. 20).

We will suddenly realize that God is doing for us what we could not do for ourselves (Big Book, p. 84).

The two friends [Bill and Dr. Bob] spoke of their spiritual experience and told him [A.A. No. 3—Bill Dotson] about the course of action they carried out (Big Book, p. 157).

You have to give it away to keep it, said the Oxford Group.[17] You have to give it away to keep it, said Sam Shoemaker.[18] And, said many AAs then and now, you have to give it away to keep it.[19] The Dead Sea, we are sometimes told, is dead because it has no outlet. So too with the message about what you yourself have done and what God has done *for* you. It must be *shared* with and for others. Sam Shoemaker said:

The Cross is a frontal attack of God upon man's pride. Its first and chief message is, "You cannot save yourself!" Salvation comes through the mercy of God, not through the merit of man. But the Cross does something else beside crushing the pride out of us. It restores us as the conscious children of God's love. Its final word is not concerned with how little we *can do* for ourselves, but with how much God *has done* for us.[20]

Do not marvel at what God has done *through* you, for you may wind up merely marvelling at you: but marvel at what God has

---

[17]Dick B., *The Oxford Group & Alcoholics Anonymous*, 2d ed., pp. 294-96, 361.

[18]See Samuel M. Shoemaker, *How to Become a Christian* (New York: Harper & Brothers, Publishers, 1953), p. 80; Dick B., *The Oxford Group & Alcoholics Anonymous*, p. 325.

[19]*Alcoholics Anonymous*, 2d ed. (New York City: Alcoholics Anonymous World Services, Inc., 1955), pp. 336-42.

[20]Samuel M. Shoemaker, Jr., *If I Be Lifted Up* (New York: Fleming H. Revell, 1931), p. 115.

done *for* you, for He has had compassion on you and is saving you unto eternal life.[21]

The very beginning of our religion is nothing we do, it is something done for us—a gift to us. Grace comes first, then character. Salvation first, then service.[22]

The message, then, was about what *had been done*, and then about giving God the credit. Shoemaker wrote:

The original Gospel was "good news." If the early Christians reached for something to say to a pagan or unbeliever in their time, they would say something about a person or an event, often about a supreme event in the life of a supreme Person such as His resurrection. . . . We must not argue, though we should be able to give good account of our faith. We shall win by witness, by simple telling of what has happened to us and to other people.[23]

This was very much what Ebby Thacher did when he carried the very first A.A. message to A.A.'s founder-to-be, Bill Wilson. Ebby looked well; he looked to Bill like he [Ebby] had been freed from alcoholism. Bill asked Ebby what had happened to him. Ebby baited the hook intended for his argumentative, drunk, atheistic friend Bill. He baited it with the Oxford Group expression, "I've got religion." Bill, as expected, became suspicious and doubting. But he had to concede to himself what he observed about Ebby's sober condition. Ebby told him what had happened in the Oxford Group, at the Calvary Mission, and why he had come fishing. Bill argued. But Ebby gave account of himself by flatly stating that God had done for him what he could not do for himself.

In his first book, Sam Shoemaker wrote:

---

[21]Shoemaker, *If I Be Lifted Up*, p. 34

[22]Shoemaker, *If I Be Lifted Up*, p. 135.

[23]*Sam Shoemaker at his best: Extraordinary Living For the Ordinary Man* (New York: Faith at Work, 1964), pp. 88-89.

Moody said, "Do not talk an inch beyond your experience," but use that for everything there is in it. It is the one thing *you* can be perfectly sure of, and you are on unassailable ground, for only yourself and God know what happened. . . . And there is no more empowering habit in the lives of those who seek to live the Christ-life than this "fishing for men," as Jesus called it. . . . Let us not forget the words of the shrewd and great-hearted Paul, that we should give "not the gospel of God only, but also our own souls," sharing our best, and not hiding our worst—humble, ernest, frank, glad, and above all loving. It is the greatest work in the world.[24]

Bill Wilson once expressed the real message in simple, yet somewhat obscure language. He painted a graphic picture. He was explaining that the answer lay in what Jesus Christ had accomplished. Jesus had done the will of his Father. Bill was illustrating a major point that Jesus had taught in the Sermon on the Mount (which Bill said contained A.A.'s basic philosophy). Jesus concluded his sermon with the teaching about doing the will of God.[25] Bill made his point by referring to what Jesus himself said to his Father in heaven, when he prayed to God in the Garden of Gethsemene.[26]

The account of what Bill did and said can be found in the story of Abby G. of Cleveland, Ohio—a Roman Catholic attorney in whose home Clarence Snyder convened the "first" meeting of Alcoholics Anonymous. Abby's personal story is titled "He thought he could drink like a gentleman" (Big Book, Third Edition, pp. 210-21). Abby wrote:

---

[24]Samuel M. Shoemaker, *Realizing Religion* (New York: Association Press, 1923), pp. 82-83.

[25]Matthew 7:21.

[26]See Matthew 26:36-44 for the account of Jesus's taking the Apostles to the "place called Gethsemane;" his sorrow; his prayer to his Father, God, asking that, if possible, "this cup pass from me;" yet concluding three times with a phrase so commonly used in A.A.: "nevertheless not as I will, but as thou *wilt . . . thy will be done.*" Mark 14:36 renders the words of Jesus as: "*nevertheless not what I will, but what thou wilt.*"

One evening I had gone out after dinner to take on a couple of double-headers and stayed a little later than usual, and when I came home Clarence [Dr. Bob's sponsee and the founder of Cleveland A.A.] was sitting on the davenport with Bill W. I do not recollect the specific conversation that went on but I believe I did challenge Bill to tell me something about A.A. and I do recall one other thing: I wanted to know what this was that worked so many wonders, and hanging over the mantel was a picture of Gethsemane and Bill pointed to it and said, "There it is" . . . (Big Book Third Edition, pp. 216-17).

Here, then, Bill Wilson—several years after he had told A.A. Number Three that the Lord had cured him of alcoholism—was telling Abby (this time, once again telling a newcomer) that the answer in A.A. lay in the accomplishments of Jesus Christ and Jesus's teaching about the importance of doing the will of God in order to obtain deliverance.

The Continued Challenge to Do God's Will

Talk the talk, but also walk the walk, people say today. It was no different in Bible times, Oxford Group times, and early A.A. The Apostles who carried the message that Jesus gave them were not educated men; they were men with experience and conviction. They had *been* with Jesus. They had seen the miracles. They were known for their love and their giving. They dedicated themselves to carrying the Word and bringing deliverance. Their message would have meant little if they had not *lived* the precepts of Jesus Christ that they had learned. Anne Smith said to early AAs: *We can't give away what we haven't got.*[27]

Dr. Bob suggested to early AAs that they read Henry Drummond's *The Greatest Thing in the World*—(love). The book would change their lives, he said.[28] Drummond's book talked

---

[27]Dick B., *Anne Smith's Journal*, 3rd ed., pp. 124-25.

[28]*Dr. BOB and the Good Oldtimers* (New York: Alcoholics Anonymous World Services, Inc., 1980), p. 310.

about the love of God and how to live it. Early AAs fervently read 1 Corinthians 13, of which Drummond's book was both study and guide. And they endeavored to live by the Corinthians definition of love. Dr. Bob called those precepts "absolutely essential."[29]

Everything about early A.A. seemed to be focussed on getting better physically, mentally, *and spiritually.* The focus was on learning the Bible and carrying to others the "good news" in the Bible's message about hope and healing. That message was carried by selfless, loving people. They were not saints, they said (even though as Christians they *were*—spiritually). But they did give of themselves. And the Big Book said at the beginning and conclusion of its basic text:

> Our very lives, as ex-problem drinkers, depend upon our constant thought of others and how we may help meet their needs (p. 20).

> Frequent contact with newcomers and with each other is the bright spot of our lives (p. 89).

> Then you will know what it means to give of yourself that others may survive and rediscover life. You will learn the full meaning of "Love thy neighbor as thyself" (p. 153).[30]

> These men had found something brand new in life. Though they knew they must help other alcoholics if they would remain sober, that motive became secondary. It was transcended by the happiness they found in giving themselves for others (p. 159).

---

[29] *Dr. BOB*, p. 96.

[30] The favorite book of the Bible in early A.A. was the Book of James, which said in James 2:8: If ye fulfill the royal law according to the scripture, Thou shalt love thy neighbor as thyself, ye do well. . .

Principles and Power

There are two aspects to "practicing the principles" that AAs
developed. The first principle necessarily had to do with
power—which is what A.A.'s Big Book declared it was all about
(3rd ed., p. 45). The second principle, necessarily dependent upon
the first, had to do with love and service.[31] Jesus delivered the
sermon on the mount which spoke much about practicing principles
of absolute love. But his *last* message was about receipt of the
spiritual power which would empower believers to be his
representatives on earth and, among other things, continue to
receive guidance and practice the principles he had taught them:

> And he said unto them, Go ye into all the world, and preach the
> gospel to every creature. He that believeth and is baptized *shall
> be saved*. . . . And these *signs shall follow them that believe*: In
> my name shall they cast out devils; they shall speak with new
> tongues; They shall take up serpents; and if they drink any
> deadly thing, it shall not hurt them; they shall lay hands on the
> sick, and they shall recover (Mark 16:15-18, emphasis added).

> Then opened he their understanding, that they might understand
> the scriptures. And said unto them, Thus it is written, and thus
> it behoved Christ to suffer, and to rise from the dead the third
> day: And that repentance and remission of sins should be
> preached in his name among all nations, beginning at Jerusalem.
> And ye are witnesses of these things. And, behold, I send the
> promise of my Father upon you: but tarry ye in the city of
> Jerusalem, until ye be *endued with power from on high* (Luke
> 24:45-49, emphasis added).

> And, being assembled together with *them*, commanded them
> that they should not depart from Jerusalem, but wait for the
> promise of the Father, which, *saith he* [Jesus], ye have heard of

---

[31]*The Co-Founders of Alcoholics Anonymous: Biographical Sketches Their Last Major
Talks* (New York: Alcoholics Anonymous World Services, Inc., 1972, 1975), p. 9.

me. For John truly baptized with water; but ye shall be baptized
with the Holy Ghost not many days hence. . . . But **ye shall
receive power**, after that the Holy Ghost is come upon you:
and ye shall be witnesses unto me both in Jerusalem, and in all
Judaea, and in Samaria, and unto the uttermost part of the earth
(Acts 1:4-5, 8, bold face emphasis added).

True to Jesus's promise, the power of the Holy Ghost did come to
the Apostles not many days thereafter (Acts 2:1-4). The apostles
spoke in tongues. *Then*, endued with power, they ministered to the
sick in the name of Jesus Christ as they had been commanded.
They lived together in fellowship. And, as the message was carried
to others, believers learned through the Church Epistles what the
Christian principles were, how to practice them, where those
believers were erring, and how to correct their errors (2 Timothy
2:15, 3:16-17).

You will note that A.A.'s Twelfth Step begins with what was
first called "conversion," then later a "religious experience," then
later a "spiritual experience," and then still later a "spiritual
awakening." But Bill Wilson boldly proclaimed the following:

Lack of power, that was our dilemma. We had to find a power
by which we could live, and it had to be a *Power greater than
ourselves* [since they had concluded that probably no human
power could help them and that they were 100% hopeless
without Divine help]. Obviously. But where and how were we
to find this Power. Well, that's exactly what this book is about.
Its main object is to enable you to find a Power greater than
yourself which will solve your problem [lack of power]. That
means we have written a book which we believe to be spiritual
as well as moral. And it means, of course, that we are going to
talk about God (Big Book, 3rd ed. p. 45).

Bill also declared, even in A.A. publications, that Ebby had
spelled out to Bill the answer—the solution—in six general ideas
that he [Ebby] applied to himself in 1934. Bill described Ebby's
sixth idea as follows:

By meditation, he sought God's direction for his life and the help to practice these principles of conduct at all times.[32]

In other words, *the alcoholic needed God's power* (received in the conversion itself and also made available in the form of revelation and guidance) for all aspects of his or her life. *And* the alcoholic needed God's power to practice the principles. There was no mention by Ebby of some "higher lightbulb" that would point the way for Bill. Power, then, was not simply the power to over-come drinking or the power that restored sanity. It was power—the gift of God—made available to believers by the grace of God to assure forgiveness, healing, deliverance, eternal life, and the ability by revelation to learn God's will, and practice the precepts in every phase of life. Calling on the Book of James, AAs said, "Faith without works is dead." But they also made it clear that works, standing alone, meant little without belief in the power of God.[33] For the Book of Ephesians, which they also studied, told them:

Wherefore I also, after I heard of your faith in the Lord Jesus, and love unto all the saints. Cease not to give thanks for you, making mention of you in my prayers. That the God of our Lord Jesus Christ, the Father of glory, may give unto you the spirit of wisdom and revelation in the knowledge of him: The eyes of your understanding being enlightened: that ye may know what is the hope of his calling, and what the riches of the glory of his inheritance in the saints. And what *is* the exceeding greatness of his power to us-ward who believe, according to the working of his mighty power (Ephesians 1:15-19).

For by grace are ye saved through faith; and that not of your-selves: *it is* the gift of God: Not of works, lest any man should boast. For we are his workmanship, created in Christ Jesus unto good works, which God hath before ordained that we should walk in them (Ephesians 2:8-10).

---

[32]*Three Talks to Medical Societies, supra*, p. 8.

[33]See also Hebrews 11:6.

4

The Golden Text of A.A. They Adopted

The Golden Text

Here is what Bill Wilson said about the "Golden Text of A.A."

Bill Wilson and Dr. Bob Smith had achieved their first success when they witnessed to a very sick attorney named Bill Dotson. Dotson was to become A.A. Number three—"the man on the bed."[1] Dotson recalled his own sense of hopelessness and despair before the visit from Dr. Bob and Bill.[2] Then, according to A.A.'s Conference Approved literature: "There was the identification with them, followed by surrendering his will to God and making a moral inventory; then, he was told about the first drink, the 24-hour program, and the fact that alcoholism was an *incurable* disease—all basics of our program that have not changed to this day."[3]

A.A.'s own account continues:

Bill D. also remembered how he was told to go out and carry the message of recovery to someone else. One of the things that

---

[1]*DR. BOB and the Good Oldtimers* (New York: Alcoholics Anonymous World Services, Inc., 1980), p. 82.

[2]*DR. BOB*, p. 83.

[3]*DR. BOB*, p. 83 (emphasis added).

really touched him was hearing Bill W. [Bill Wilson] tell Mrs. D. [Bill Dotson's wife] about a week later, "Henrietta, the *Lord* has been so wonderful to me *curing me* of this terrible disease, that I just want to keep talking about it and *telling people*."[4]

Note carefully: We are talking about A.A. *Number One* (Bill Wilson). Bill Wilson was talking about *the Lord*. Bill Wilson was declaring that *the Lord had cured him of his disease. Cured*! And Bill Wilson wanted to keep talking about it and telling people (*witnessing to the cure*).

That is the message this booklet is designed to carry. God can, does, and will cure. God can, does, and will heal. And Bill Wilson specifically stated that God *did* cure him. Bill and Bob told A.A. Number Three to "go out and carry the message of recovery to someone else." Then Bill Wilson himself *did* tell Bill Dotson's wife (Henrietta) of the *cure*. And Bill's witnessing had a great impact on Bill Dotson. For Dotson pronounced Bill Wilson's words as the *golden text of A.A.* Dotson said in his personal story in A.A.'s basic text:

> We [Bill Wilson, Bill Dotson, and Dotson's wife, Henrietta] were eating lunch, and I was listening and trying to find out why they had this release that they seemed to have. Bill looked across at my wife, and said to her, "Henrietta, *the Lord has been so wonderful to me, curing me of this terrible disease*, that I just want to keep talking about it and telling people" (Big Book Third Edition, p. 191, emphasis added).

> I [Bill Dotson] thought, "I think *I have the answer*." Bill [Wilson] was very, very grateful that he had been released from this terrible thing and he had given God the credit for having done it, and he's so grateful about it he wants to tell other people about it. That sentence, "*The Lord has been so wonderful to me, curing me of this terrible disease*, that I just want to keep telling people about it," has been a sort of a

---

[4]*DR. BOB*, p. 83 (emphasis added).

golden text for the A.A. program and for me (Big Book Third Edition, p. 191).

As Christian believers, AAs Could Claim Power through Accepting Christ

During his presence here on earth, Jesus wielded the power of God to accomplish signs, miracles, and wonders. He also gave his seventy disciples power:

Behold, I give you power to tread on serpents and scorpions, and over all the power of the enemy: and nothing shall by any means hurt you (Luke 10:19).

To believers, Jesus said:

Verily, verily, I say unto you, He that believeth on me, the works that I do shall he do also; and greater *works* than these shall he do; because I go unto my Father. And whatsoever ye shall ask in my name, that will I do, that the Father may be glorified in the Son (John 14:12-13).

After he had been crucified, lain in the grave for three days and three nights, and been raised by God from the dead, Jesus stood in the midst of the apostles and those that were with them and then declared:

And, behold, I send the promise of my Father upon you: but tarry ye in the city of Jerusalem, until ye be endued with power from on high (Luke 24:49).

And, being assembled together with *them*, commanded them that they should not depart from Jerusalem, but wait for the promise of the Father, which, *saith he*, ye have heard of me (Acts 1:4)

But ye shall receive power, after that the Holy Ghost is come
upon you:and ye shall be witnesses unto me . . . (Acts 1:8).

On the day of Pentecost, the apostles *did* receive the promised
power (Acts 2:1-4). They spoke in tongues. They began healing in
the name of Jesus Christ (Acts 3:6, 16; 4:10). And they, along
with other believers, began preaching the availability of salvation,
and using the power of God, in the name of their Lord Jesus
Christ; and the Bible states:

And with great power gave the apostles witness of the
resurrection of the Lord Jesus; and great grace was upon them
all (Acts 4:33).

And by the hands of the apostles were many signs and wonders
wrought among the people . . . (Acts 5:12).

[Peter said] Neither is there salvation in any other; for there is
none other name under heaven [than that of Jesus Christ of
Nazareth] given among men, whereby we must be saved (Acts
4:12)

Jesus Promised God's Power to
All Who Believed, Saying:

. . . Go ye into all the world, and preach the gospel to every
creature. He that believeth and is baptized shall be saved . . .
And these signs shall follow them that believe: In my name
shall they cast out devils . . . they shall lay hands on the sick,
and they shall recover. . . . And they went forth, and preached
every where, the Lord working with *them*, and confirming the
word with signs following. Amen (Mark 16:15-28, 30).

And when Paul, the Apostle to the Gentiles, received revelation
that the power was available to *all* believers—Jew and Gentile
alike—he wrote:

. . . . The word is nigh thee, *even* in thy mouth, and in thy heart: that is, the word of faith which we preach: That if thou shalt confess with thy mouth the Lord Jesus, and shalt believe in thine heart that God hath raised him from the dead, thou shalt be saved (Romans 10:8-9).

For I am not ashamed of the gospel of Christ: for it is the power of God unto salvation to every one that believeth; to the Jew first, and also to the Greek (Romans 1:16).

For the preaching of the cross is to them that perish foolishness; but unto us which are saved it is the power of God (1 Corinthians 1:18).

But we have this treasure in earthen vessels, that the excellency of the power may be of God, and not of us (2 Corinthians 4:7).

The Pioneers Claimed Receipt of That Power

There is no mystery about what early AAs studied in the Bible. That history has simply become clouded with errors, omissions, and deletions. But the author's books show what Bill Wilson, Dr. Bob Smith, Anne Smith, Henrietta Seiberling, T. Henry Williams, and Clarace Williams said about the subjects studied. And what they said is further clarified by the very detailed references to Scripture that can be found in the books, sermons, articles, and papers of Wilson's teacher Sam Shoemaker. The Book of James was mentioned, but not explained by A.A. itself. The same is true of Corinthians, the sermon on the mount, the Book of Acts, the Church Epistles, Psalms, Proverbs, and the other segments mentioned by the founders. The concepts about power mentioned in the foregoing Bible verses were not strange to the pioneers. Anne Smith pointed out that Paul himself realized that a power stronger than his was needed.[5] And the early A.A. surrenders

---

[5]Dick B., *Anne Smith's Journal, 1933-1939: A.A.'s Principles of Success*, 3rd ed. (Kihei, HI: Paradise Research Publications, Inc., 1998), p. 22.

upstairs at T. Henry's home and also in Dr. Bob's home very closely resembled the following account in the Book of James—the A.A. favorite:

> Is any sick among you? let him call for the elders of the church; and let them pray over him, anointing him with oil in the name of the Lord: And the prayer of faith shall save the sick, and the Lord shall raise him up; and if he have committed sins, they shall be forgiven him. Confess your faults one to another, and prayer for one another, that ye may be healed. The effectual fervent prayer of a righteous man availeth much (James 5:14-16).[6]

Giving God the Glory

If the surrender of self to God, and reliance upon the power of God are important, as we have shown above, it is equally important that God be given the credit. That *is* the message. Bill Wilson gave God the credit, specifically emphasizing the Lord's curing him. A.A. Number Three continued to give God the credit through the Golden Text of A.A. Dr. Bob said: "Your Heavenly Father will never let you down" (Big Book Third Edition, p. 181)! And once again God was given the credit. This was Biblical too:

> For this cause I bow my knees unto the Father of our Lord Jesus Christ. That he would grant you, according to the riches of his glory, to be strengthened with might by his Spirit in the inner man; That Christ may dwell in your hearts by faith. . . . (Ephesians 3:14-17).

> Now unto him that is able to do exceeding abundantly above all that we ask or think, according to the power that worketh in us. Unto him *be* glory in the church by Christ Jesus throughout all ages, world without end. Amen (Ephesians 4:20-21).

---

[6]See Dick B., *The Akron Genesis of Alcoholics Anonymous*, 2d ed (Kihei: HI: Paradise Research Publications, Inc., 1998), pp. 72-74, 176-78, 188-97, 218-22.

Whether therefore ye eat, or drink, or whatsoever ye do, do all
to the glory of God (1 Corinthians 10:31).

Expressing Gratitude through Deed and Word

The heart of the early A.A. program was working unselfishly for
others. The Book of James was their favorite book of the Bible,
they said.[7] And they adhered to two ideas in James, as Sam
Shoemaker had taught, and as Dr. Bob and Bill had told Bill
Dotson to do:

> But be ye doers of the word, and not hearers only, deceiving
> your own selves. For if any be a hearer of the word, and not a
> doer, he is like unto a man beholding his natural face in a glass:
> For he beholdeth himself, and goeth his way, and straightaway
> forgetteth what manner of man he was. But whoso looketh into
> the perfect law of liberty, and continueth *therein*, he being not
> a forgetful hearer, but a doer of the work, this man shall be
> blessed in his deed (James 1:22-25).

> What *doth it* profit, my brethren, though a man say he hath
> faith, and have not works? Can faith save him? If a brother or
> sister be naked and destitute of daily food, And one of you say
> unto them, Depart in peace, be *ye* warmed and filled; notwith-
> standing ye give them not those things which are needful to the
> body; what *doth it* profit? Even so faith, if it hath not works, is
> dead, being alone (James 2:14-17).

Faith without works is dead! This is a frequently used and adapted
phrase from the Bible in A.A.'s Big Book, even today.

---

[7]*Pass It On* (New York: Alcoholics Anonymous World Services, Inc., 1984), p. 147.

5

The Critical Need
to Seek God Again Today

This booklet is not intended as a salvation tract. It is intended to show that the alcohol and drug scene—with all the government money, all the law enforcement effort, all the advertisements, all the coalitions, all the treatment centers, all the counselors, and all the statistics—is a sorry scene at best. Scientists and scholars and case workers may argue over which is best—"group therapy *and* renewed church attendance *and* disulfiram and vocational rehabilitation." Or they may agree with the author of the foregoing quote who also said, "There is no single, best, or only treatment for alcoholism, and it is easier to walk with two crutches than one."[1] That author, the distinguished Dr. George E. Vaillant, concludes that all the treatment modes should be used *together*. Yet this is almost exactly where the treatment of alcoholism was when A.A. was founded. At that point, there was little progress. Doctors shook their heads. Treatment was ineffective. And the drunks turned to God. Why not today—again!

---

[1]George E. Vaillant, *The Natural History of Alcoholism Revisited* (Cambridge, MA: Harvard University Pres, 1995), p. 369.

Self-help Will Not Cut It. That Is Not a Solution.

Three points need to be made about what has come to be known as the "self-help" program or "solution" of present-day Alcoholics Anonymous, other Twelve Step groups, and "group therapy." Whether "self-help" or "mutual help" provide the answer to addiction and alcoholism we leave to others to debate. But *self-help in no way describes the early A.A. answer.* So let's take a good, long look at what the differences were.

First, early A.A. had to do with Divine help, not self help. The First Edition of A.A.'s Big Book gives an opinion said to have been held by "Many doctors and psychiatrists, including 'One of these men, staff member of a world-renowned hospital' who said:

> As to two of you men, whose stories I have heard, there is no doubt in my mind that you were *100% hopeless, apart from Divine help.* Had you offered yourselves as patients at this hospital, I would not have taken you, if I had been able to avoid it. People like you are too heartbreaking. Though not a religious person, I have profound respect for the spiritual approach in such cases as yours. *For most cases, there is virtually no other solution*" (Big Book, First Edition, pp 54-55, emphasis added).

Corroborating this statement, by pointing to his friend and "sponsor" Ebby Thacher, Bill wrote:

> *Doctors had pronounced him incurable.* Society was about to lock him up. Like myself, he had admitted complete defeat (Big Book, First Edition, p. 21, emphasis added).

Second, early A.A. concerned God-sufficiency, not self-sufficiency. Bill wrote in the chapter designed to persuade atheists and agnostics:

> When we saw others solve their problems by simple reliance upon the *Spirit* of this universe, we had to stop doubting the

power of God. Our ideas did not work. But the God idea did (Big Book, First Edition, p. 65, emphasis added).[2]

We agnostics and atheists were sticking to the idea that self-sufficiency would solve our problems. When others showed us that *"God-sufficiency"* worked with them, we began to feel like those who had insisted the Wrights would never fly (Big Book, First Edition, p. 65, emphasis added).[3]

God had restored his sanity. . . . Even so has God restored us all to our right minds (Big Book, First Edition, p. 69).[4]

Third, the self-help idea had been repudiated long before A.A. began. A.A.'s spiritual teacher, the Reverend Sam Shoemaker said the gospel of "self help" needs to be cured and corrected by faith in what Jesus Christ accomplished for mankind by his crucifixion, burial, and resurrection.[5]

Finally, when applied in the A.A. setting: (1) The "self-help" idea flaunts early A.A.'s renunciation of reliance on self and human power; (2) Its total inadequacy—as a single idea or as part of collective ideas proposed by Dr. Vaillant—simply underlines the necessity today for reliance upon the power of God.

Medical Help and Psychological Help Have Not Cut It

In the author's new title, *New Light on Alcoholism: God, Sam Shoemaker, and A.A.*, an appendix has been added to show the present state of opinion and present statistics on recovery (or,

---

[2]For the Bible's statement that God is Spirit, see John 4:24.

[3]For the Bible's references to the sufficiency of God, see 2 Corinthians 3:5; 9:8.

[4]2 Timothy 1:7: For God hath not given us the spirit of fear; but of power, and of love, and of a sound mind.

[5]Samuel M. Shoemaker, Jr., *If I Be lifted Up* (New York: Fleming H. Revell, 1931), p. 167.

better, lack of it). The facts are as alarming as they are overwhelming.[6]

The Four Early A.A. Factors Needed Today

Early A.A. went through three developmental stages. First, it relied upon the Bible and the principles of the Oxford Group. Second, as time went on, it may have developed six steps to utilize the principles that would provide the Pioneers with the power of God, the guidance of God, and the goodness of God by which they could stay in harmony with God's will.

The author believes the *essential* ingredients that were present in early A.A. can be reduced to four in number. These ingredients, we believe, suggest how to get back to God, how to rely on God, and how to stay *within* the important A.A. program of drunks helping drunks to find God and get well and live a happy and productive life. There is certainly no assurance that A.A. as a society will today, ever return to God, to the Bible, or to Christianity.

There certainly is a very real possibility for a change that will answer three pressing calls: (1) The call of many Christians in today's "self-help" anonymous groups who are despairingly awash. (2) The call of those within the groups who are frequently being intimidated to back away from Christ, or those who might well come to Christ within those groups except for the intimidating objections to the mention of anything biblical or Christian. (3) The call of those who are turning to other Christian groups, proliferating in number, with less time for drunks, less identification with drunks, less experience in alcoholism, less focus on just alcoholism or drug addiction, and, in many cases, far less success than that demonstrated by the early A.A. successes rate.

---

[6]Dick B., *New Light on Alcoholism: God, Sam Shoemaker, and Alcoholics Anonymous*, 2d ed. (Kihei, HI: Paradise Research Publications, Inc., 1999), Appendix Twelve.

Lots today are quibbling with, explaining away, or simply denying the statement that early A.A. had a 75% to 93% success rate among those who really tried. But the statements—quite frequently made within and outside of A.A.—are either true or false. In 1958, Bill Wilson addressed the New York City Medical Society on Alcoholism. The subject was *Alcoholics Anonymous—Beginnings and Growth*. Speaking of the period from 1939 to 1941, Bill told the physicians:

> As we gained size, we also gained in effectiveness. The recovery rate went way up. Of all those who really tried A.A., a large percent made it at once, others finally made it; and still others, if they stayed with us, were definitely improved. Our high recovery rate has since held, even with those who first wrote their stories in the original edition of "Alcoholics Anonymous." In fact, 75 per cent of these finally achieved sobriety. Only 25 per cent died or went mad. Most of those still alive have now been sober for an average of twenty years.[7]

Speaking of the period from 1939 forward, when A.A. was growing like wild-fire in Cleveland, A.A.'s own official biography of Dr. Bob said: *"Records in Cleveland show that 93 percent of those who came to us never had a drink again"* (emphasis added)[8]

The following, the author believes, are the four essential and biblical ingredients which can be replicated today and *revitalize the golden text of A.A.*

First, A Fellowship of Those Needing Help

Fellowship is a Biblical principle that is stressed in the Book of Acts. The early Christians fellowshipped together in their homes. They fellowshipped together daily. They prayed together. They studied the Word of God together daily. They broke bread

---

[7]*Three Talks to Medical Societies*, *supra*, p. 13. See Big Book, 3rd ed., p. xx.

[8]*DR. BOB and the Good Oldtimers* (New York: Alcoholics Anonymous World Services, Inc., 1980), p. 261.

together daily. And they witnessed together. As the result of such daily fellowship (as recorded in the Book of Acts), literally thousands came to believe. They concluded they needed God and came to Him through His son Jesus Christ. Many sought healing and were healed.

In its own humble and limited way, early A.A. was not that much different. AAs became Christians or returned to Christianity. Their fellowships took place in the homes. As one historian observed, the pioneers' lives seemed to consist of one continuous meeting. They prayed together. They studied the Bible together. They often broke bread together. And they reached out to newcomers together. The Big Book pointed out that this alone would not have held them together; instead the fellowship provided the backdrop for agreed *common* solution upon which they had agreed to *join in brotherly and harmonious action* (Big Book, First Edition, p. 27). However, that brotherly and harmonious group was, in the beginning: A fellowship of *believers* who (1) Concurred in their belief in God; (2) Studied His Word to learn how to gain access to Him; (3) Read devotionals and Christian literature to help them understand Him better and practice His presence; and (4) Relied upon Him for forgiveness, healing, deliverance, guidance, and abundance. And there is no reason whatever why believers or potential believers in today's A.A. should not be free and comfortable to do this again—within A.A. itself. Bill Wilson wrote approvingly to Father John Ford, S.J. about the prevalence of Roman Catholic retreats for AAs. He wrote approvingly to his friend and teacher Sam Shoemaker about the possibility for A.A. Bible study groups. What has happened to A.A.'s links to religion?

In A.A. today, there are atheist groups. There are loners. There are gay and lesbian groups. There are women's groups. There are men's stag groups. There are groups for pilots, young people, the deaf, doctors, and lawyers. And there should be no index of forbidden books which prevents or dissuades or intimidates Bible study groups.[9] Bill Wilson expressed no dissent over Roman Catholic groups. Nor did he object to Eastern Religion groups. He even told Sam Shoemaker it would be interesting to see a Bible study group of AAs. And where has this liberality gone today? Akron A.A. was described in terms of "old fashioned prayer meetings" with Bible study, prayer, and the frequent use of a Methodist quarterly. There was no particular prejudice against the Bible in early Cleveland A.A. Its bulletins regularly referred to the Bible. Yet one group in the southern United States was expelled from the official meeting schedule for studying, of all people, Emmet Fox and his *The Sermon on the Mount*. There is even a strong move afoot to eliminate the Lord's Prayer at the conclusion of meetings.

Second, a Healing and Cure by God Almighty

Despite anything anyone can say today, the early AAs were helpless, hopeless, and powerless. They had tried self-knowledge, will-power, and lots of human powers. But they were adjudged "medically incurable" and 100% hopeless apart from "Divine help." They based their hopes, efforts, and achievements on a cure by God Almighty. In one A.A. publication, a famous medical writer observed:

> The average AA wouldn't know a hormone from a hole in the ground; he'd flunk any medical school exam on the cause of alcoholism. How then do the AAs get to be the great alcohol doctors that they unquestionably are? The answer is as simple as it is rugged—every AA has to first nearly die of the disease of which he becomes the master physician. The medicine the AAs use is unique. Though it should be all-powerful, it has never been tried with any consistent success against any other major sickness. This medicine is no triumph of chemical science; has needed no billion dollar scientific foundation to

---

[9]See Dick B., *That Amazing Grace: The Roles of Clarence and Grace S. in Alcoholics Anonymous* (San Rafael, CA: Paradise Research Publications, 1996).

discover it; does not come in capsules or syringes. It is free as
air—with this provision: that *the patients it cures* have to nearly
die before they can bring themselves to take it. *The AAs'
medicine is God and God alone. This is their discovery*
(emphasis added).[10]

Many years earlier, Morris Markey had set the alcoholic
"medicine" in a much appreciated spotlight. Markey wrote an
article for *Liberty* that received lots of attention and produced lots
of inquiries about the miraculous program.[11] Markey's title was
Alcoholics and God. The bold-face lead said:

**Is there hope for habitual drunkards? A cure that borders
on the miraculous—and it works!**[12]

Here are some excerpts from the Markey's account:

Perhaps you are one of those cynical people who will turn away
when I say that the root of this new discovery is religion.

[Telling the story of Bill Wilson, Wilson's hot-flash experience,
and Dr. Silkworth] "Well, doc," he said, "my troubles are all
over. I've got religion." "Why, you're the last man" [said Dr.
Silkworth]. "Sure, I know all that. But I've got it. And I know
I'm cured of this drinking business for good" [said Wilson].

Here is how it works: Every member of the group—which is to
say every person who has been saved—is under obligation to
carry on the work, to save other men. That, indeed, is a
fundamental part of his own mental cure.

---

[10]Paul de Kruif, *Volume II: Best of The Grapevine* (New York: The AA Grapevine,
Inc., 1986), pp. 202-03.

[11]See the comments of Bill Wilson in *Alcoholics Anonymous Comes of Age* (New
York: Alcoholics Anonymous World Services, Inc., 1957), pp. 177-78. At page 177:
"To our great delight, Morris soon hammered out an article which he titled "Alcoholics
and God.""

[12]*Liberty Magazine*, September, 1939, p. 6.

Even though the man [the newcomer] might be an atheist or agnostic, he will almost always admit there is some sort of force operating in the world—some cosmic power weaving a design. And his new friend will say: "I don't care what you call this Somebody Else. We call it God."

But the patient *can* have enough confidence in God—once he has gone through the mystical experience of recognizing God. And upon that principle the Alcoholic Foundation rests.

In 1939, at about the same time, Dr. Harry Emerson Fosdick wrote a book review of A.A.'s basic text, *Alcoholics Anonymous*. It had been solicited by AAs. The review was later placed by Bill Wilson in A.A.'s own history.[13] Fosdick said:

The core of their whole procedure is religious. Agnostics and atheists, along with Catholics, Jews, and Protestants, tell their story of discovering the Power greater than themselves. "WHO ARE YOU TO SAY THAT THERE IS NO GOD," one atheist in this group heard a voice say when, hospitalized for alcoholism, he faced the utter hopelessness of his condition. . . . They agree that each man must have his own way of conceiving God, but of God Himself they are utterly sure. . . .

In the decade of research he has done on this subject, the author corresponded with Dr. Norman Vincent Peale several times. Finally, shortly before Dr. Peale's death, the author had an hour's visit with the noted clergyman. Peale recounted the number of times he had met with Bill Wilson. Then the author asked Dr. Peale who the "Higher Power" in A.A. actually was. Peale replied that he had never heard one single person who did not agree that the "Higher Power" was God. Of course, the Big Book itself makes this clear on pages 43 and 100 of its Third Edition. But Peale pointed the author to his book, *The Power of Positive*

---

[13]*Alcoholics Anonymous Comes of Age: A Brief History of A.A.* (New York: Alcoholics Anonymous World Services, Inc., 1957), pp. 322-23.

Thinking.[14] There, Dr. Peale—a good friend of both Bill Wilson and A.A.—wrote:

> When he [a member of Alcoholics Anonymous] accepts this point of view [that he has no power within himself; that he is defeated] he is in a position to receive help from other alcoholics and from the Higher Power—God (p. 268).

> But I [Peale quoting his friend Charles who was cured of alcoholism] drew upon a Higher Power and the Higher Power, which is God, did it (p. 272).

> Your problem may not be alcoholism, but the fact that the Higher Power can heal a person of this most difficult malady emphasizes the tremendous truth related in this chapter and throughout the entire book that there is no problem, difficulty, or defeat that you cannot solve or overcome by faith, positive thinking, and prayer to God. The techniques are simple and workable. And God will help you always . . . (p. 275).

It defies common sense and the intelligence level of almost anyone in A.A.—including the sickest—to expect a desperate alcoholic to pray to a chair, a lightbulb, or a group and be cured of alcoholism. AAs may be sick. *They are not stupid!* Even more, A.A. today has had crammed into its rooms people from enormously diverse sources: Courts, parole offices, probation offices, correctional institutions, treatment centers, therapists, physicians, clergymen, non-profit agencies, and even government agencies. Its newcomers include men and women who are atheists, agnostics, New Age advocates, Satan worshippers, airline pilots, homosexuals, lesbians, blacks, hispanics, orientals, lawyers, Eskimos, Native Americans, Roman Catholics, Protestants, Jews, and a sprinkling of Moslems, Hindus, and people espousing other Eastern religions.

---

[14]Norman Vincent Peale, *The Power of Positive Thinking* (New York: Peale Center for Christian Living, 1952).

Does this diversity require or make it any more likely that such people will swallow a doorknob as the object of their prayers? Atheists and Roman Catholics and Native Americans and hispanics are no more stupid as a group than AAs themselves. Plainly—and again—*none is stupid*!

Early AAs relied on God. God! Not a lightbulb, nor a doorknob, nor a tree. Nor an "it!" They relied upon God. That was their "medicine." It worked! So said Paul de Kruif in A.A.'s own publication; and rightly so. It is a fact. In fact it is *the* fact that made A.A. so attractive when it was producing miracles.

Third, a Program That Changes Lives

The Oxford Group people were called Life Changers. They said they had a life-changing program. And they sought to change lives by conversion to Jesus Christ, followed by a life pointed toward living by his standards. They also claimed that each of their principles, including their own four absolute standards, came from the Bible.

The average A.A. newcomer of yesteryear and of today arrives at his or her first meeting saddled with *inappropriate* behavior. And that is putting it mildly! The Oxford Group people, Sam Shoemaker, and Anne Smith (Dr. Bob's wife) referred to a prayer applicable to the unmanageability of *any* newcomer's life: "O God, Manage me because I cannot manage myself." A.A.'s First Step thus suggests an admission and conclusion that AAs cannot manage their own lives. Perhaps a crude, but better way to put it, would be: When they have managed their own lives, they have either screwed up, or screwed their lives up further by sedating their failures with overpowering amounts of booze. The same for addicts.

Jesus Christ specialized in offering a changed life—not just through healing, but through believing, salvation, forgiveness, and frequent challenges to practice the great commandments love. Early AAs liked Jesus's sermon on the mount. They liked Paul's 1 Corinthians 13. And they especially liked the Book of James.

They proclaimed these Bible segments to be "absolutely essential" to their program. And each one of these Bible portions—based on the power of Christ for believers—urged principles of love that are very demanding for the average believer, or any person. Yet they recognized that God expects something other than idol worship, immoral behavior, selfishness, retaliation, envy, and so on.

Every fearless and searching A.A. Fourth Step is almost sure to unearth endless resentments, fears, dishonesty, and selfishness. It may not be that the alcoholic is uniquely bad. For sure, he or she inherits the old man nature in all of us:

> But ye have not so learned Christ; If so be that ye have heard him, and have been taught by him, as the truth is in Jesus. That ye put off concerning the former conversation the old man, which is corrupt according to the deceitful lusts. And be renewed in the spirit of your mind (Ephesians 4:20-23).

> If ye then be risen with Christ, seek those things which are above, where Christ sitteth on the right hand of God. Set your affections on things above, not on things on the earth. For ye are dead, and your life is hid with Christ in God. . . . Mortify therefore your members which are upon the earth; fornication, uncleanness, inordinate affection, evil concupiscence, and covetousness, which is idolatry. . . . In the which ye also walked some time, when ye lived in them. But now ye also put off all these; anger, wrath, malice, blasphemy, filthy communication out of your mouth. Lit not to one another, seeing that ye have put off the old man with his deeds; And have put on the new man, which is renewed in knowledge after the image of him that created him (Colossians 3:1-10).

Liquor distorts behavior, adjustments, thinking, and responses. Taken in excess, it hardly contributes to sane or sound or reasonable thoughts. If the old man nature prevails, and if it is messed up with too much liquor, and if the mind itself becomes short-circuited, a miserable life seems guaranteed. And alcoholism loves misery. It produces it. It subtly promises relief from it. Then it aggravates it. And finally it beclouds the misery and becomes the believed, but completely illusory, solution to it.

A changed life in the alcoholic, which asks God for relief from the insanity of too much drink and then asks for relief from the things that lead to drink and then asks for instructions as to how to line one's life up with the will of God, is a life that early AAs sought.

Neither an higher power, nor a light bulb, nor a random group of court-ordered newcomers, is likely to produce the change. On the other hand, Oxford Group people from Calvary Protestant Episcopal Church in New York in the 1930's *followed the Rev. Sam Shoemaker from his church to Madison Square bearing the sign: Jesus Christ changes lives. And William Griffith Wilson was in that very procession!*[15] Presumably to experience a life change and then witness to it.

Fourth, a Message of Victory to Carry

The message that had impact when Jesus was walking the earth was the message that people had seen signs, miracles, and wonders: The dead were raised. The lame walked. The blind were given sight. The dumb spoke. The deaf heard. People flocked to those gatherings—even the people who opposed Jesus.

The message that had impact when the Apostles were walking the earth in the First Century was that the Apostles also were performing the same signs, miracles, and wonders that Jesus Christ did—just as he had promised they could and would after they became endued with power.

This was a message that had impact when people were willing to believe that healing was available even after Jesus Christ and the First Century Christians had departed this earth. Even in churches,

---

[15]The author has a photo of this procession. Bill Wilson's friend, L. Parks Shipley, Sr., told the author that he had marched in such a procession and that Bill Wilson had been one of the marchers on occasion.

missions, Twelve Step programs, treatment centers, and jails.[16] For some reason, this is a message that scientists, government statisticians, treatment people, and even clergy often seem reluctant to embrace. One scholarly religious writer said, for example:

> Healing of addiction through the supernatural intervention of the Holy Spirit outside of twelve-step recovery programs is rare.[17]

We disagree. Shoemaker's own Rescue Mission produced healings. The Salvation Army produced healings.[18] There are countless examples of healings today on television. And our booklet has been about specific healings that were needed, were sought, and were obtained from God Almighty in Alcoholics Anonymous. The author's own case is one of these.

Jesus urged his followers to become fishers of men.[19] Paul urged Christians to be Ambassadors for Christ.[20] The Bible urged all believers to preach the good news and promised that God would confirm His word with signs following.[21]

Carry the message. Receive the blessing. You have to give it away to keep it, said the AAs and the Oxford Group. A better way to express it might be: You have to give it away to *get* it or at least to experience it.

---

[16]Compare the astonishing story of Frank Costantino, whom the author has come to know personally. Frank Costantino: *Holes in Time: The Autobiography of a Gangster*, 2d ed. (Dallas: Acclaimed Books, 1986). Also, Jerry G. Dunn, *God Is for the Alcoholic* (Chicago, Moody Press, 1965).

[17]Terry Webb, *Tree of Renewed Life: Spiritual Renewal of the Church through the Twelve-Step Program* (New York: Crossroad, 1992), p. 113.

[18]Harold Begbie, *Twice Born Men: A Clinic in Regeneration* (New York: Fleming H. Revell, 1909).

[19]Matthew 4:19: And he saith unto them, Follow me, and I will make you fishers of men. See also *Sam Shoemaker at His Best* (New York: Faith at Work, Inc., 1964), p. 86.

[20]2 Corinthians 5:20: Now then we are ambassadors for Christ, as though God did beseech *you* by us: we pray *you* in Christ's stead, be ye reconciled to God.

[21]Mark 16:14-20.

6

Two Challenges for Real Spirituality Today

The Challenges

The author's most recent major title is *New Light on Alcoholism: God, Sam Shoemaker, and A.A.*[1] This new work studies all of Sam Shoemaker's contributions to A.A. It particularly highlights in one chapter two particular ideas that Sam pushed in his parish at Pittsburgh during the eve of his long and distinguished career.

Sam Urged That Pittsburgh Be As Famous for God As It Was for Steel

We urge: that the Twelve Steps once again become as famous for bringing people to God as they have become for "self-help" and reliance upon some curious "higher power."

---

[1]Dick B., *New Light on Alcoholism: God, Sam Shoemaker, and A.A.* (Kihei: HI: Paradise Research Publications, Inc., 1999).

Sam Urged: Get Changed. Get Together. And Get Going

We urge: that A.A. opt today for more effective results; and we believe these can flow within the rooms of A.A. and restore God, the Bible, and Christianity to their rightful place in the original and miraculous history of early A.A.

- Get changed — Once again, That A.A. Put God first!

- Get together — That AAs Agree: Reliance on God *Was* First!

- Get Going — Tell It Accurately: *God* Could and *Did* When Sought!

The Real Meaning of "Spirituality" in Early A.A. and for Today

What a diversity of confused ideas one can hear about "spirituality" today. You hear it with reference to "New Age" ideas. You hear it with reference to Bible ideas. You hear it with reference to moral principles. You hear it in supposed contradistinction to "religion." You hear it with reference to "imperfection" and "not-godedness." And you hear it when you haven't the slightest idea what the speaker or writer *is* talking about.

One talented and effective A.A. writer, with long-term sobriety and many articles in A.A. publications to his credit, wrote:

AA members have always issued disclaimers when discussing God: Typical is, "Our program is spiritual, not religious." If pressed for what the program's actual definition of *spiritual* is, however, it's doubtful that many AA members could explain.[2]

We don't agree with the first part of that writer's observation. We do most certainly agree with the second: Most A.A.'s haven't any idea at all what the real meaning of "spirituality" is. And we don't think it's their fault. Everyone and his uncle has taken a crack at the word "spiritual;" and it seems that few if any have taken a good look at the First Edition of the Big Book and what Bill Wilson there said about real spirituality. In today's A.A., with the original and now three revised Big Book editions under its belt—each edition eliminating more and more of the personalities and even some of the significant language of early A.A.—it seems less and less likely that the rank and file AAs of today will understand the emphasis on God that existed in A.A.'s first four years.

Spirituality in the Big Book, First Edition: Dependence upon Our Creator

Bill Wilson wrote:

> We never apologize to anyone for depending upon our Creator. We can laugh at those who think spirituality the way of weakness. Paradoxically, it is the way of strength. The verdict of the ages is that faith means courage. All men of faith have courage. They trust their God. We never apologize for God (p. 81).

---

[2]Mel B., *New Wine: The Spiritual Roots of the Twelve Step Miracle* (Center City, MN: Hazelden, 1991), p. 5.

Spirituality in the Big Book, Third Edition:
Trusting and Relying upon God

Bill Wilson wrote:

> Perhaps there is a better way—we think so. For we are now on
> a different basis; the basis of trusting and relying upon God. We
> trust infinite God rather than our finite selves (p. 68).

Spirituality in the Bible:
Trust in God

One favorite set of verses in Proverbs that was important to early
AAs was:

> Trust in the Lord with all thine heart; lean not unto thine own
> understanding. In all thy ways acknowledge him, and he shall
> direct thy paths (Proverbs 3:5-6).

There is another from Psalms:

> I sought the Lord, and he heard me, and delivered me from all
> my fears. . . . This poor man cried, and the Lord heard *him*,
> and saved him out of all his troubles (Psalms 34:4, 6).

Trusting God Almighty Isn't Easy, but
Look What It Did for Early AAs

One might say that there must have been great need for the
voluminous revelation from God that is called the "Word of God,"
the "Bible," and, in early A.A., "The Good Book." God wanted
a family—children. It started with Adam and Eve, and so did
trouble when the Devil began his importuning. Man needed a
savior. It started with Jesus, and so did trouble when the Devil
fashioned the death of the son of God. Man needed victory. It
started with the Book of Acts when man saw what God had really
done to assure his overcoming the works of the Devil.

The Bible talked of this. Shoemaker talked of this. And early AAs talked of it. They needed victory over an almost assured death from alcoholism—a death that seems even more assured when people today mix their alcoholism with every other conceivable form of addiction. The victory was accomplished by Jesus Christ, as Bill Wilson and Bill Dotson so well pointed out in their golden text. But the victory required work. The pioneers often quoted the book of Romans:

> I beseech you therefore, brethren, by the mercies of God, that ye present your bodies a living sacrifice, holy, acceptable unto God, *which is* your reasonable service. And be not conformed to this world: but be *ye* transformed by the renewing of your mind, that ye may prove what *is* that good, and acceptable, and perfect, will of God (Romans 12:1-2).

The pioneers also studied the epistles of John:

> For whatsoever is born of God overcometh the world: and this is the victory that overcometh the world, *even* our faith. Who is he that overcometh the world, but he that believeth that Jesus is the Son of God (1 John 5:4-5).

A Biblical Look at the Golden Text of A.A.

A word or two from the Apostle, Peter:

> Then Peter opened *his* mouth, and said, Of a truth I perceive that God is no respecter of persons: But in every nation he that feareth him, and worketh righteousness is accepted with him. The word which *God* sent unto the children of Israel, preaching peace by Jesus Christ: (he is Lord of all:) That word, *I say*, ye know, which was published throughout all Judaea, and began from Galilee, after the baptism which John preached; How God anointed Jesus of Nazareth with the Holy Ghost and with power: who went about doing good, and healing all that were oppressed of the devil; for God was with him (Acts 10:34-38).

[Explaining the healing at the temple gate] And as the lame man which was healed held Peter and John, all the people ran together unto them in the porch that is called Solomon's, greatly wondering. And when Peter saw *it*, he answered unto the people, Ye men of Israel, why marvel ye at this? or why look ye so earnestly on us, as though we by our own power or holiness we had made this man to walk? The God of Abraham, and of Isaac, and of Jacob, the God of our fathers, hath glorified his Son Jesus; whom ye delivered up. . . . And his name through faith in his name hath made this man strong whom ye see and know: yea, the faith which is by him hath given him this perfect soundness in the presence of you all (Acts 3:11-16).

A word or two from Bill Wilson:[3]

The god of intellect displaced the God of our fathers. But again John Barleycorn had other ideas. We who had won so handsomely in a walk turned into all-time losers. We saw that we had to reconsider or die (pp. 29-30).

When we encountered A.A., the fallacy of our defiance was revealed. At no time had we asked what God's will was for us; instead we had been telling Him what it ought to be. No man, we saw, could believe in God and defy Him, too. Belief meant reliance, not defiance (p. 31).

God will restore us to sanity if we rightly relate ourselves to Him (p. 33).

Real spirituality in early A.A. and in A.A. today means believing in and relying upon God Almighty. In early A.A., it meant coming to Him through His son. The strength of A.A. by itself lies in one alcoholic who has been cured telling another alcoholic that he can be cured. The weakness comes when God is left out of the picture.

---

[3]Twelve Steps and Twelve Traditions (New York: Alcoholics Anonymous World Services, Inc., 1952).

One drunk does the talking. The next drunk does the listening. Identification occurs. God is presented as the solution. The way to come to God is prescribed. The need to harmonize one's life with God's will is prescribed as the path. Abolition of self-centeredness, self-sufficiency, and self-aggrandizement is explained as the price. And a life of peace, freedom, and joy can be promised. Can this become available in today's A.A. for those who want it. We think so if they learn and know where they came from.

Paul wrote the Galatians:

> Stand fast therefore in the liberty wherewith Christ hath made us free, and be not entangled again with the yoke of bondage. . . . For in Jesus Christ neither circumcision availeth any thing, nor uncircumcision; but faith which worketh by love (Galatians 5:1-6).

Bill Wilson was not afraid to tell this story. Bill Dotson was not afraid to make it his own golden text and call it the golden text for A.A. On the other hand, Dr. Bob had been telling the story all along when he called Akron A.A. and every single meeting in Akron a "Christian Fellowship." Why then should AAs today continue to be afraid to speak of their own golden beginnings and their own successful formula for a cure?

The End

About the Author

Dick B. writes books on the spiritual roots of Alcoholics Anonymous. They show how the basic and highly successful biblical ideas used by early AAs can be valuable tools for success in today's A.A. His research can also help the religious and recovery communities work more effectively with alcoholics, addicts, and others involved in Twelve Step programs.

The author is an active, recovered member of A.A.; a retired attorney; and a Bible student. He has sponsored more than seventy men in their recovery from alcoholism. Consistent with A.A.'s traditions of anonymity, he uses the pseudonym "Dick B."

He has had fourteen titles published: *Dr. Bob and His Library*; *Anne Smith's Journal, 1933-1939*; *The Oxford Group & Alcoholics Anonymous: A Design for Living That Works*; *The Akron Genesis of Alcoholics Anonymous*; *The Books Early AAs Read for Spiritual Growth*; *New Light on Alcoholism: God, Sam Shoemaker, and A.A.*; *Courage to Change* (with Bill Pittman); *The Good Book and The Big Book: A.A.'s Roots in the Bible*; *That Amazing Grace: The Role of Clarence and Grace S. in Alcoholics Anonymous*; *Good Morning!: Quiet Time, Morning Watch, Meditation, and Early A.A.*; *Turning Point: A History of Early A.A.'s Spiritual Roots and Successes*, *Hope!: The Story of Geraldine D., Alina Lodge & Recovery*, *Utilizing Early A.A.'s Spiritual Roots for Recovery Today*, and *By the Power of God: A Guide to Early A.A. Groups & Forming Similar Groups Today*. The books have been the subject of newspaper articles, and have been reviewed in *Library Journal*, *Bookstore Journal*, *For a Change*, *The Living Church*, *Faith at Work*, *Sober Times*, *Episcopal Life*, *Recovery News*, *Ohioana Quarterly*, *The PHOENIX*, *MRA Newsletter*, and the *Saint Louis University Theology Digest*.

Dick is the father of two married sons (Ken and Don) and a grandfather. As a young man, he did a stint as a newspaper reporter. He attended the University of California, Berkeley, where he received his A.A. degree, majored in economics, and was elected to Phi Beta Kappa in his Junior year. In the United States Army, he was an Information-Education Specialist. He received his A.B. and J.D. degrees from Stanford University, and was Case Editor of the Stanford Law Review. Dick became interested in Bible study in his childhood Sunday School and was much inspired by his mother's almost daily study of Scripture. He joined, and was president of, a Community Church affiliated with the United Church of Christ. By 1972, he was studying the origins of the Bible and began traveling abroad in pursuit of that subject. In 1979, he became much involved in a Biblical research, teaching, and fellowship ministry. In his community life, he was president of a merchants' council, Chamber of Commerce, church retirement center, and homeowners' association. He served on a public district board and was active in a service club.

In 1986, he was felled by alcoholism, gave up his law practice, and began recovery as a member of the Fellowship of Alcoholics Anonymous. In 1990, his interest in A.A.'s Biblical/Christian roots was sparked by his attendance at A.A.'s International Convention in Seattle. He has traveled widely; researched at archives, and at public and seminary libraries; interviewed scholars, historians, clergy, A.A. "old-timers" and survivors; and participated in programs on A.A.'s roots.

The author is the owner of Good Book Publishing Company and has several works in progress. Much of his research and writing is done in collaboration with his older son, Ken, who holds B.A., B.Th., and M.A. degrees. Ken has been a lecturer in New Testament Greek at a Bible college and a lecturer in Fundamentals of Oral Communication at San Francisco State University. Ken is a computer specialist.

Dick is a member of the American Historical Association, Maui Writers Guild, and The Authors' Guild. He is available for conferences, panels, seminars, and interviews.

Dick B.'s Historical Titles on Early A.A.'s Spiritual Roots and Successes

Dr. Bob and His Library: A Major A.A. Spiritual Source (Third Edition)
Foreword by Ernest Kurtz, Ph.D., Author, *Not-God: A History of Alcoholics Anonymous*.
A study of the immense spiritual reading of the Bible, Christian literature, and Oxford Group books done and recommended by A.A. co-founder, Dr. Robert H. Smith. Paradise Research Publications, Inc.; 156 pp.; 6 x 9; perfect bound; $15.95; 1998; ISBN 1-885803-25-7.

Anne Smith's Journal, 1933-1939: A.A.'s Principles of Success (Third Edition)
Foreword by Robert R. Smith, son of Dr. Bob & Anne Smith; co-author, *Children of the Healer*.
Dr. Bob's wife, Anne, kept a journal in the 1930's from which she shared with early AAs and their families ideas from the Bible and the Oxford Group. Her ideas substantially influenced A.A.'s program. Paradise Research Publications, Inc.; 180 pp.; 6 x 9; perfect bound; 1998; $16.95; ISBN 1-885803-24-9.

The Oxford Group & Alcoholics Anonymous (Second Edition)
Foreword by Rev. T. Willard Hunter; author, columnist, Oxford Group activist.
A comprehensive history of the origins, principles, practices, and contributions to A.A. of "A First Century Christian Fellowship" (also known as the Oxford Group) of which A.A. was an integral part in the developmental period between 1931 and 1939. Paradise Research Publications, Inc.; 432 pp.; 6 x 9; perfect bound; 1998; $17.95; ISBN 1-885803-19-2. (Previous title: *Design for Living*).

The Akron Genesis of Alcoholics Anonymous (Newton Edition)
Foreword by former U.S. Congressman John F. Seiberling of Akron, Ohio.
The story of A.A.'s birth at Dr. Bob's Home in Akron on June 10, 1935. Tells what early AAs did in their meetings, homes, and hospital visits; what they read; how their ideas developed from the Bible, Oxford Group, and Christian literature. Depicts roles of A.A. founders and their wives; Henrietta Seiberling; and T. Henry Williams. Paradise Research Pub.; 400 pp., 6 x 9; perfect bound; 1998; $17.95; ISBN 1-885803-17-6.

The Books Early AAs Read for Spiritual Growth (Fwd. by John Seiberling; 7th Ed.)
The most exhaustive bibliography (with brief summaries) of all the books known to have been read and recommended for spiritual growth by early AAs in Akron and on the East Coast. Paradise Research Publications, Inc.; 126 pp.; 6 x 9; perfect bound; 1998; $15.95; ISBN 1-885803-26-5.

New Light on Alcoholism: God, Sam Shoemaker, and A.A. (2d Ed.)
Forewords by Nickie Shoemaker Haggart, daughter of Rev. Sam Shoemaker; and Mrs. W. Irving Harris.
A comprehensive history and analysis of the all-but-forgotten specific contributions to A.A. spiritual principles and practices by New York's famous Episcopal preacher, the Rev. Dr. Samuel M. Shoemaker, Jr.—dubbed by Bill W. a "co-founder" of A.A. and credited by Bill as the well-spring of A.A.'s spiritual recovery ideas. Paradise Research Publications, Inc.; 672 pp.; 6 x 9; perfect bound; 1999; $24.95; ISBN 1-885803-27-3.

The Good Book and The Big Book: A.A.'s Roots in the Bible (Bridge Builders Ed.)
Foreword by Robert R. Smith, son of Dr. Bob & Anne Smith; co-author, *Children of the Healer*.
The author shows conclusively that A.A.'s program of recovery came primarily from the Bible. This is a history of A.A.'s biblical roots as they can be seen in A.A.'s Big Book, Twelve Steps, and Fellowship. Paradise Research Publications, Inc.; 264 pp.; 6 x 9; perfect bound; 1997; $17.95; ISBN 1-885803-16-8.

That Amazing Grace: The Role of Clarence and Grace S. in Alcoholics Anonymous
Foreword by Harold E. Hughes, former U.S. Senator from, and Governor of, Iowa.
Precise details of early A.A.'s spiritual practices—from the recollections of Grace S., widow of A.A. pioneer, Clarence S. Paradise Research Pub; 160 pp.; 6 x 9; perfect bound; 1996; $16.95; ISBN 1-885803-06-0.

Good Morning!: Quiet Time, Morning Watch, Meditation, and Early A.A. (2d Ed.)
A practical guide to Quiet Time—considered a "must" in early A.A. Discusses biblical roots, history, helpful books, and how to. Paradise Research Pub; 154 pp.; 6 x 9; perfect bound; 1998; $16.95; ISBN: 1-885803-09-5.

Turning Point: A History of Early A.A.'s Spiritual Roots and Successes
Foreword by Paul Wood, Ph.D., President, National Council on Alcoholism and Drug Dependence.
Turning Point is a comprehensive history of early A.A.'s spiritual roots and successes. It is the culmination of six years of research, traveling, and interviews. Dick B.'s latest title shows specifically what the Twelve Step pioneers borrowed from: (1) The Bible; (2) The Rev. Sam Shoemaker's teachings; (3) The Oxford Group; (4) Anne Smith's Journal; and (5) meditation periodicals and books, such as *The Upper Room*. Paradise Research Publications, Inc.; 776 pp.; 6 x 9; perfect bound; 1997; $29.95; ISBN: 1-885803-07-9.

Inquiries, orders, and requests for
catalogs and discount schedules
should be addressed to:

Dick B.
c/o Good Book Publishing Company
P.O. Box 837
Kihei, Maui, Hawaii 96753-0837
1-808-874-4876 (phone & fax)
email: dickb@dickb.com

Internet Web Site: "http://www.dickb.com"

Order Form

Qty.

Send: ___ *By the Power of God: A Guide to Early A.A.*   @ $16.95 ea. $____
            Groups & Forming Similar Groups Today

            Paradise Research Publications, Inc.; 258 pp.; 6 x 9; perfect
            bound; 2000; ISBN: 1-885803-30-3.

    ___ *Utilizing Early A.A.'s Spiritual Roots for Recovery*   @ $14.95 ea. $____
            Today

            Paradise Research Publications, Inc.; 106 pp.; 6 x 9; perfect
            bound; 1999; ISBN: 1-885803-28-1.

    ___ *The Golden Text of A.A.: God, the Pioneers, and*   @ $14.95 ea. $____
            Real Spirituality

            Paradise Research Publications, Inc.; 94 pp.; 6 x 9; perfect
            bound; 1999; ISBN: 1-885803-29-X.

                                      Subtotal $_____

Shipping and Handling (within the U.S.)   Shipping and Handling $_____
     Add 10% of retail price (minimum $3.75)
                                    Total Enclosed $_____

Name: _____ (as it appears on your credit card, if using one)

Address: _____   E-mail: _____

City: _____ State: ____ Zip: _____

CC Acct. #: _____ **Circle:** MC VISA AMEX Exp. ____

Tel.: _____ Signature _____

Please mail this Order Form, along with your check or money order, to: Dick B., c/o Good Book Publishing Company, P.O. Box 837, Kihei, HI 96753-0837. Please make your check or money order payable to "**Dick B.**" in U.S. dollars drawn on a U.S. bank. Please contact us for Shipping and Handling charges for orders being shipped outside of the United States. If you have any questions, please phone or fax: 1-808-874-4876. Dick B.'s email address is: dickb@dickb.com. The "**Dick B. [Internet] Web Site on Early A.A.**": "http://www.dickb.com".

How to Order Dick B.'s Historical Titles on Early A.A.

Order Form

Qty.

Send:

___ *Turning Point* (a comprehensive history)	@ $29.95 ea.	$_____
___ *New Light on Alcoholism* (Sam Shoemaker)	@ $24.95 ea.	$_____
___ *The Oxford Group & Alcoholics Anonymous*	@ $17.95 ea.	$_____
___ *The Good Book and The Big Book* (Bible roots)	@ $17.95 ea.	$_____
___ *The Akron Genesis of Alcoholics Anonymous*	@ $17.95 ea.	$_____
___ *That Amazing Grace* (Clarence and Grace S.)	@ $16.95 ea.	$_____
___ *Good Morning!* (Quiet Time, etc.)	@ $16.95 ea.	$_____
___ *Anne Smith's Journal, 1933-1939*	@ $16.95 ea.	$_____
___ *Books Early AAs Read for Spiritual Growth*	@ $15.95 ea.	$_____
___ *Dr. Bob and His Library*	@ $15.95 ea.	$_____

Shipping and Handling (S & H) **   Subtotal $_____

Add 10% of retail price (minimum US$3.75). ** U.S. only.
For "The Set," add US$18.67. ** U.S. only   **S & H** $_____
Please call, fax, or email for shipments outside the U.S.

Total Enclosed $_____

Name: _____ (as it appears on your credit card)

Address: _____

City: _____ State: ___ Zip: _____

Credit Card #: _____ (MC VISA AMEX) **Exp.** _____

Tel. #: _____ Signature _____

Email address: _____

Special Value for You!

If purchased separately, the author's ten titles sell for US$191.50, plus Shipping and Handling. Using this Order Form, you may purchase sets of all ten titles for **only US$149.95 per set, plus US$19.15** Shipping and Handling. Please contact us for Shipping and Handling charges for orders being shipped outside of the United States.

Send Order Form (or copy), with check or money order, to: Dick B., P.O. Box 837, Kihei, HI 96753-0837. Please make check or money order payable to "**Dick B.**" in U.S. dollars drawn on a U.S. bank. For questions, please phone or fax: 1-808-874-4876. Our email: dickb@dickb.com. **Dick B.'s Web Site**: "http://www.dickb.com".